George Sanders was born in St Petersburg in 1906. He left Russia in 1917 with his family, who settled in England and had George educated at Bedales and Brighton College.

He made his British film debut in 1929, but it was in 1930's Hollywood that he honed his distinctive, charming-yet-dangerous screen persona – the quintessential cad. Sanders co-starred in Alfred Hitchcock's *Rebecca* and *Foreign Correspondent* (both 1940), and went on to win an Academy Award for his signature role, that of Addison DeWitt in *All About Eve* (1950). He continued to work in films up until the year of his death in 1972.

In the 1940's, Sanders' film-star status was the impetus for his two crime novels, both featuring recognizably Sanders-esque heroes: *Crime on My Hands* (1944) and *Stranger at Home* (1946). In 1960 came a third book: his autobiography, fittingly titled *Memoirs of A Professional Cad* in which the line between fiction and fact is blurred even more convincingly – and wittily – than in the novels.

George Sanders

Memoirs of
A Professional Cad

DEAN STREET PRESS

This book is affectionately dedicated to my father, who is the source of my past experience, and to Benita, who is the sauce of my present laughter.

G. S.

Also by George Sanders

Crime on My Hands
Stranger at Home

BOOK I

CHAPTER 1

On JULY 3, 1906, the world was at peace. Nothing of any consequence seemed to be happening in the capital cities of any of its countries. Nothing disturbed the summer lethargy of its population. Everywhere people dozed contentedly, unaware that an event of major importance was taking place in St. Petersburg, Russia. At number 6 Petroffski Ostroff, to Margaret and Henry Sanders, a son of dazzling beauty and infinite charm was being born. It was I.

I emerged somewhat reluctantly from my mother's womb at 6 o'clock in the morning. My father, who had been warned of the impending event only a short time prior to its occurrence, had rushed off to get the midwife who lived across the Neva on the Vassilsky Ostroff. He drove in a droshky to the Toochkoff Bridge, a wooden bascule, or draw, bridge, which was opened sometimes in the summer to let the river traffic through. It was opening when he reached it. Alighting from

the carriage and disregarding the warning cries of the boat-
men, he leapt across the widening gap and ran the rest of the
way to the midwife's house. He brought her back across the
river in a rowboat, and in a state of exhaustion, pushed her
into my mother's room, where she accomplished a successful
delivery.

In the light of the fact that I have been supporting my
father for the past twenty years, his concern for my welfare at
the time of my birth would appear to have been thoroughly
justified.

I was born into a world that was soon to disappear. It was
a world of clinking champagne glasses, of colonnaded private
ballrooms with scintillating chandeliers, of heel-clicking bemonocled princes in gorgeous uniforms intent upon their
ladies as they drove in their jingling troikas through the
moonlit snow.

A world that was not to be recreated for forty years—and
then by M-G-M in Cinemascope with Fernando Lamas.

My parents were not members of the nobility nor were they
terribly rich. But like most people seemed to be in those days,
they were well-off. They were both born in St. Petersburg
but were not orthodox Russians, since their ancestors came
from Scotland. My mother was descended through her grand-
mother from the Thomas Clayhills of Dundee, who went to
Estonia in 1626 to establish a business there. Thus it was from
forebears of solid social position and impeccable respectabil-
ity that my mother came.

To the best of my knowledge, my father came in the mail.

We had a summer house in Estonia at a place called Hun-
gerburg. In common with its neighbors, it had a large ve-
randa overlooking the beach.

Mixed bathing was not allowed, since everybody swam or
paddled in the nude. Men and women went into the water in

shifts controlled by the position of a pennant attached to a tall flagpole that dominated the beach.

When the pennant was down it was the men's turn. When it was raised the men would come out of the water and disappear into their respective beach-house enclosures.

Then, timorously, casting wary looks to right and left, and crossing their arms across their breasts to clothe their nudity, the women would tiptoe out of their cabañas and, gaining courage with every step, make their way down to the water's edge where they would dunk themselves like so many doughnuts, squealing with sensual delight, secure in the conviction that they were not being observed.

Meanwhile, the men would take up their favorite positions on the verandas, whence they watched these activities through high-powered binoculars.

In this manner a commendable degree of decorum was preserved within an atmosphere of genteel concupiscence.

And my own instruction in anatomy, though frequently interrupted by the importunities of my nurse, was initiated on a solid foundation.

Many of our winters were spent on an estate we had acquired across the Finnish border at a place called Mustamäki.

While in the grounds of our town house in St. Petersburg we had a private skating rink and a couple of artificially built-up toboggan runs, in Mustamäki the whole countryside, blanketed with crisp, sparkling snow, lay open to us for skiing, skijoring and riding *spaakstotin*.

There was the incomparable, invigorating air scented by the pine trees. There was the ice-yachting on the frozen lake. There were the high-speed sleighs, drawn by diminutive fast-running Finnish ponies, their bridles hung with merrily jingling bells.

The estate was to prove a godsend when the time came for my parents to flee from the Bolshevik revolution.

When I look back on my childhood it seems to me that all of my activities consisted in swimming, canoeing, sailing, skiing, toboganning, skating and listening to my father play the balalaika.

My father was regarded as the best amateur balalaika player in St. Petersburg. He was in fact the co-discoverer of the instrument with the celebrated Andreyeff. Previously the balalaika was known only to country folk who used it for accompanying their village choirs. Andreyeff and my father brought the instrument to St. Petersburg and together they had a lot of successful soirées in fashionable circles. It was at one of these that my mother met my father for the first time and became fascinated by his balalaika.

She was a woman of great beauty, as well as being an heiress to a modest fortune, a fact which struck as responsive a chord in my father as any that he could pluck from his bizarre-looking instrument.

It was inevitable that a number of balalaika concerts later they were married.

The concerts continued. Andreyeff and my father became the rage of St. Petersburg. In the course of time word of their virtuosity reached the Imperial family and they were invited to perform at court. Their debut at the vast castellated palace at Gatchina that was the summer residence of Tsar Alexander III was so successful they were given medals and decorations of a size and of an order of magnificence that would have turned Douglas Fairbanks positively green with envy.

I myself was being taught the violin, but I could not see myself winning any medals at it, so I chucked it. My interest lay in sport, in fun and in games, and of these I had plenty.

If it is true that a man's character develops for the good

in proportion to the fun, the degree of happiness and the amount of bountiful love he experiences in childhood, then I must have the most noble and wonderful character in all the world. Personally, I feel that I am the living proof of this contention. However, a surprising number of people think otherwise.

At all events, until the day that my mother took me to school in England my life seemed to be nothing but fun. I remember having an odd feeling on the day we left St. Petersburg that we would never return. As it turned out, we never did. It was this poignant moment of leave-taking that was also my closest brush with history.

Sir Winston Churchill touched unwittingly upon this moment of my life when he wrote of certain events that were taking place in 1917:

> In the middle of April the Germans took a sombre decision . . . they turned upon Russia the most grisly of all weapons. They transported Lenin, in a sealed truck, like a plague bacillus from Switzerland into Russia.

Lenin was going in as I was coming out. At the Finland Station in St. Petersburg he was being met by his pals Joe Stalin, Kamenev, Zinoviev, Trotsky and the rest of the Bolshevik gangsters.

I was being seen off by my father, my Uncle Frederick in his scarlet Cossack uniform, my Aunt Margaret, Prince and Princess Erivansky, Count Benkendorff and my Cousin Agnes.

Lenin was arriving full of plans for my money. I was leaving for school in England, serenely unaware of his existence.

To the rest of our gay and well-to-do gathering, Lenin and his fellow conspirators were just a bunch of rather badly behaved peasants.

Lenin's plans were not confined to the appropriation of the trust funds that various affluent uncles and aunts of mine had set up to insure for me the sort of life that would have suited my indolent nature—they were far more comprehensive. They included everybody else's money as well. They also included the murder of most of my relatives.

I must confess that there are times when I wish they had included the murder of all of them. However, I think I might have spared the ones that provided for me. Quite frankly, I am sorry about the money. I would have liked to have had it.

On March 15, 1917, in the drawing room of his special train which had been immobilized at Gatchina by the revolutionaries, the Tsar received Minister of War Guchkow, and right-wing Deputy, Basil Shulgin. They induced him to sign a document which read in part: *In agreement with the Imperial Duma, we have thought it good to abdicate from the Throne of the Russian State and to lay down the Supreme Power . . .*

Unbeknown to my family and myself at the time, in signing this document the Tsar had signed away our inheritances, our holdings and our gilt-edged future, an action for which I, personally, have never forgiven him.

Anyway, it was not long after this that the revolution got started in earnest.

It erupted like an angry boil that had been squeezed too soon, its skin becoming red and inflamed, its poisonous pus spreading over the face of Russia, contaminating all but the well-to-do, who languidly turned a blind lorgnette upon it.

Incredible though it may seem, in corrupt, fun-loving St. Petersburg life went on the same as before. In private ballrooms and fashionable restaurants the effete nobility, immaculately attired in their colorful uniforms, toasted one another in vodka and Crimean champagne, while gypsy orchestras played the Mazurka, the Polka, and the Waltz. Gambling for high stakes in the clubs continued uninterruptedly, unaffected by the shooting that was going on outside.

The supply of, and the demand on, the services of the hard-working prostitutes remained in fine balance.

The great Karsavina danced to spellbound audiences at the Mariinsky Theatre.

Chaliapin still sang.

One of the great heroes of my childhood, my Uncle Jack, contentedly pursued one of his favorite pastimes. From his great carved bed, a .22-caliber pistol in his hangover-shaking hand, he would shoot flies that had gathered to eat the jam he had smeared on the ceiling. Liveried footmen stood by with champagne, extra rounds of ammunition, orange marmalade and strawberry jam.

Outside in the streets men were dying for a cause to which they were passionately attached, and did not really understand. A cause which only specious dialectics sought to explain.

In the houses of the rich, men were dying in a different way. Desuetude had signed their death warrants, they were incapable of believing that anything serious was happening.

No one took any notice of the fact that on April 2, 1917, President Wilson spoke of "The wonderful and heartening things that have been happening in the last few weeks in Russia." American sentiment was solidly on the side of the revolutionaries.

The very next day, April 3rd, Kerensky's provisional government was granted credits by the U. S. A. amounting to $325,000,000.

For this modest sum America not only guaranteed the success of the revolution, she also bought herself a lifelong enemy, to defend herself against whom it has cost her untold billions of dollars and a tax burden as onerous as that of 1776.

The Tsar certainly had at his disposal the means with which to subdue the revolutionaries. But he didn't have the heart.

In 1917 woolen-heartedness seemed to be the order of the day, for in far-off peaceful Hampshire, my mother received a letter from my father in which he said that there were no signs of the threatened revolution and that it was perfectly safe for her to return and join him in St. Petersburg.

This she did, having left my brother and myself in the care of English relatives.

Not long after her arrival in St. Petersburg, the situation became untenable. My mother and father had to flee for their lives across the ice to Mustamäki whence they eventually made their way to England. All of their possessions were left behind and were never recovered.

The Tsar and his family were shot, along with most of our relatives and friends.

My Uncle Bob got a job playing the cello in a cinema in Finland, and eventually became a professor of biology in Sweden.

My Uncle Jack became a professional house guest until his welcome wore thin. Then he became a guest in the wrong sort of houses until in the end he died of syphilis on the Riviera.

My grandfather escaped to Switzerland, where he was able to live in great comfort while at the same time providing financial support not only to my family but also to our surviving relatives, whose number was fortunately not great enough to put a strain on his resources.

He was able to do this by virtue of having had investments in Wall Street which lasted until the crash in 1929.

Not long after this greatest of all our catastrophes it became my lot to assume his mantle of responsibility and to give rather than to receive. It was no surprise to me to discover that the former set of conditions was infinitely more blessed than the latter.

Although we made good our escape from Russia in a physical and economic sense, in a psychological sense no escape was possible. The mechanisms at work within the minds of White Russians which prevented them from accepting the reality of the revolution when it started, also prevented them from accepting it as an immutable *fait-accompli* when they became its refugees.

Even today after forty-one years of uninterrupted communist rule, the Bolshevik revolution has not been fully accepted by White Russians.

My father has never wavered from his conviction that in the course of time Russia will go back to what he calls normal and that he will get all his property back. He is today, at the age of ninety, in active negotiation for the return of our house in St. Petersburg.

Among the White Russians in Paris and elsewhere the habit of living in the past became just as deeply ingrained. Consequently, aptitudes and talents were enfeebled, and opportunities to start a new life tragically neglected. So much time was spent in thinking and talking about the past, that there was little time for the present. Consequently though Russian refugees were glamourous and deeply sympathized with at first, their inability to adjust to their situation became in the course of time an irksome bore to their friends, and an insoluble problem to themselves. A young Russian refugee I know in California told me how much he missed Paris, and how he longed to go back. "Well, why don't you?" I asked him. "I'm afraid of the Russians," he said. "You mean you think they'll move in and take over

Europe?" I asked him. "Good Lord, no," he said. "I'm afraid of the *White* Russians."

It is perhaps interesting to note that even the most gifted, the most virtuous, or those most assiduously addicted to the practice of common sense are all equally at the mercy of the almighty booby trap of circumstance. It makes little difference whether one is kicked upstairs or down, the adjustment is hard to make. The essential requirement is flexibility and the ability to improvise.

Football-pool winners and impoverished refugees are often found in the same boat. It is not the degree of ill or good fortune that seems to matter. It is the sudden change that unseats people.

Of course all this has been said before in many different ways and by many different people. Perhaps it has never been said better than by W. Somerset Maugham when he wrote:

> In other arts proficiency can be obtained, but in life little more can be done than to make the best of a bad job. Art is an effect of design: life is so largely controlled by chance that its conduct can be but a perpetual improvisation.

CHAPTER 2

DUE TO CIRCUMSTANCES well within
their control but not within the scope of their knowledge,
my parents sent me to the wrong schools. They did what
most if not all parents do, for the appropriate method of
educating any individual can only be determined in retro-
spect. Environment, atavistic tendencies and inherited talents
create needs which are not always catered to by institutions
of learning. These needs may lie dormant in an individual
repressed by fear of failure to conform. Years later, they
manifest themselves in various ways, but by then it is usually
too late, the individual has become a square peg in a round
hole and the burden of responsibility he has acquired in the
meantime is too heavy for him to set aside.

In my own case I feel that I am gradually succeeding in
re-educating myself to the point I should have arrived at
thirty years ago, and, if I live long enough, I may be able
to catch up with myself.

The first school I was sent to was called Bedales. It was a coeducational school, set in beautiful surroundings near Petersfield in Hampshire. The teachers were both male and female, the atmosphere permissive, the food good, the beds comfortable, the discipline lax. One did not learn very much, but boys and girls sat together at desks-built-for-two and some of the girls were very pretty and it was rather fun.

One day every other week, usually Friday, was called a "free day." It was a day on which each student could choose his own curriculum, that is, within reason. They were not allowed to choose pure idleness as of course most would have wished to do, but they were allowed to work in the workshops, which many of them did, and they were also allowed to choose a girl partner and go for a picnic ramble through the woods. This was the form of activity that I personally favored, though I used to wonder sometimes if the educational theories we put into practice on these occasions coincided with those of the school authorities. However, my instinct told me that it would be imprudent to inquire. On Saturday nights there was dancing in the great hall, dark corners of which were decorated with mistletoe.

The permissive nature of this educational system did not, however, extend to the point of sanctioning some of my brother's activities. On one occasion when a master was gently reminding him that it was time for classes, my brother saw fit to intimidate him with a loaded revolver and was promptly expelled. Shortly after this unfortunate incident my parents decided to remove me from Bedales and send me to the same school that my brother was to attend—Brighton College.

It was with infinite sadness that I said farewell to my girl friends, the comfortable beds, the well-cooked meals, the indulgent teachers, the mistletoe and the beautiful scenery of Hampshire.

Now began four years of poor food, uncomfortable beds, sordid scenery, irascible, acidulated teachers, frequent beatings, no girls, no fun, nothing but pimply-faced boys of all shapes and sizes.

A rough-and-tumble bunch they were, the flotsam and jetsam of lower middle-class families, congregated in the cloistered, austere and somewhat moth-eaten atmosphere of a second-rate public school, of which they were incongruously proud. Proud of an institution dedicated to prepare them to be square pegs in round holes, an institution which sponsored the diurnal practice of informing the boys from the pulpit of the school chapel that they were sinners, and the nocturnal practice of beating them with canes to bring about a measure of their redemption; an institution whose main purpose seemed to be that of convincing the boys that they were dunces. I, myself, was a poor student, partly because it was the fashion and partly because the efforts of the teachers to convince me that I was a dunce were highly successful, as were also their efforts to convince me that I was a sinner.

When I finally left the school after four years of manufacturing cigarettes out of blotting paper, which we smoked at the back of the classroom, playing practical jokes on masters and boys alike, and generally excelling at totally unnecessary activities such as football and cricket, I left with a sense of utter worthlessness and the conviction that I was too stupid to cope with life.

Looking back across the thirty-five years that have elapsed since that memorable day, I must confess that little has happened in my life to make me feel justified in altering that opinion. Sometimes, when my spirits are depressed, I get the strong feeling that when I meet my teachers in the next world I shall be able to tell them that after all they were right.

CHAPTER 3

T HE FIRST JOB I got after I left school was in a textile-producing company in the grimy city of Manchester. It was a job for which, even if I had been able to get the hang of my duties, I could not have demonstrated any aptitude, nor engendered any genuine interest.

I can only assume that my motive in getting it in the first place sprang from an adolescent desire to prove to my parents, whom I had persuaded to let me leave school, that I was capable of supporting myself. I proved the reverse. My salary was only two pounds a week, on which of course I could not live, and which therefore had to be supplemented by an allowance from home. It was a relief to everyone including myself when after a year of this fruitless activity I was good-naturedly thrown out of the company.

My next job, which I got through the lack of influence of my father, was with a cigarette-manufacturing company in Argentina. I worked for a while in the factory in Buenos Aires, and after that I was sent into the provinces and eventually to Patagonia to compile a survey.

The company wanted to know what the people of Patagonia were smoking, and whether they could be induced to smoke the company's brand. I had little heart for the latter part of my mission since I felt that whatever they were smoking would be an improvement on what I had to sell them.

From Buenos Aires I traveled to Ingeniero Jacobacci, where the railroad came to an end and one had his choice of proceeding south on foot, on horseback or in a model-T Ford, following barely discernible wagon tracks. Choosing the model-T, I bribed an Indian guide who spoke Guarani, the native language, to accompany me into the wilds.

And wilds they were. There were virtually no roads, no electricity, and no hotels. The custom in that part of the world at that time was that travelers would be bedded and fed, free of charge, at privately owned sheep ranches which, though few and far between, were the only means of shelter available. However, hospitality was only extended if one arrived before sundown. Because of the numerous, hardworking bandits in this area, the ranchers had a discouraging habit of opening fire with Winchester rifles on anyone approaching their property after dark.

But the traveler arriving before the sun had set, and because he was a potential bringer of news and gossip to a community which had no other means of obtaining it, was welcomed with open arms and inexhaustible hospitality. He could stay as long as he wanted to, and never be expected to pay a farthing.

It occurred to me at the time that by choosing his route carefully, a man could make a career of visiting sheep ranches in Patagonia. In fact I was tempted to abandon my survey and embark upon such a venture myself, but finally, and somewhat reluctantly, decided against it.

Naturally enough we tried to reach one of those ranches each day before sundown, but on many occasions this was not possible, and we would have the tantalizing experience of getting within sight of a ranch just as it grew dark. On these occasions we would camp where we were, first digging a circular trench and filling it with the dried dung of the guanaco—a llamalike animal which abounds in Patagonia—and then lighting the dung, which would smolder all night, serving the dual purpose of keeping us warm and frightening off the wild animals.

The guanaco, incidentally, is a paradoxical beast. Although it has many of the temperamental deficiencies of the camel, such as a proclivity for spitting and biting, it can be domesticated and then becomes docile enough to answer to its name.

Because these creatures destroy the ranchers' crops, the Government had put a two-dollar bounty on each guanaco head brought in. I often wondered why, in view of the ease with which the animals could be tamed, someone had not set himself up with a guanaco "ranch," corraling and domesticating a few hundred of the creatures, and then lopping off a dozen or so heads for the bounty whenever he had need of spending money.

After three months in the wilds, I began making my way from ranch to ranch back to civilization.

Patagonia has a stark, moonlike topography. It is dusty and lonely, and there is a constant, irritating wind that whistles right through you.

Buenos Aires was to me, on my return, an entirely new world. After my primitive existence in Patagonia, I was in perfect health and savored everything I saw and experienced.

I remember standing on a corner of the Plaza de Mayo,

my mouth hanging open like some country bumpkin, staring at the myriad bright lights of the city, the sleek powerful cars, the elegantly dressed women. For a full two weeks this wonderful feeling, almost like being born again, invested all of my activities. I was sharply aware of the worried faces of the men who hurried by me on the street, carrying the inevitable brief cases. They, on the other hand, seemed to notice nothing around them.

After months of nearly total abstinence, one martini would make me quite lightheaded.

So it was that from this experience I arrived at the conclusion that to enjoy one's life to its fullest, one must build contrast into it. And the more extreme the contrast the fuller the life.

I had thoroughly enjoyed my travels through the wilds of Patagonia, where at times I felt almost like an animal. My senses became more acute, and I virtually glowed with good health. I lived and ate simply and slept soundly. The robust state of health I was in and the kind of life I was leading would produce in me an appetite so ravenous that I would drool at the mouth like a wild beast at the mere smell of food.

It was the custom around sundown for a couple of ranch hands to go out among the sheep and pick out a succulent-looking lamb. They would isolate this animal from the rest of the herd and then quickly, with a skill born of years of practice, plunge a knife into a vital part so that it would die immediately with neither the herd, nor itself, having sensed danger and thereby spoiling the meat by a surge of adrenalin, as happens in slaughterhouses.

The lamb would be brought back, skinned and prepared for the spit, and would be roasting only a few minutes later.

We would sit in a circle around the turning spit, while a gourd of *hierba mate,* from which we would all drink in turn through a *bombilla,* was passed around. Finally, the roast done, the ranch owner would turn to the guest and offer him the honor of the first cut. I would draw my knife and cut myself the choicest piece and then return to the circle, where I would eat it with my fingers as was the custom.

The combination of my ravenous appetite and this tender, pure meat, eaten in the open air, produced a gastronomical sensation which no restaurant in the world could ever hope to provide.

On the other hand, when I returned to Buenos Aires I enjoyed the city just as much. It became a new experience for me. I found, though, that this heightened appreciation of civilized life eventually wore thin and only a normal interest remained.

In order to enjoy life to its fullest, one should not have too much of either the primitive or the civilized life. We all need periods of living as nearly like an animal as possible. Even living in discomfort if necessary.

I am a man who loves his comfort devoutly, but I realize that to appreciate comfort to the full I must have periods without it. Whenever I make a motion picture on location, this need is thoroughly satisfied.

Most people can attain this contrast in living during their annual holidays though few take advantage of the opportunity. They will not find it where they usually seek it—in a holiday spent at a seaside resort or in a populous area.

One should live for a time as close to the soil as possible with virtually no intellectual activity. Books, radios and all creature comforts should be left at home. Merely changing the scenery doesn't make for much of a holiday, especially if one continues to do the same things. I remember once boarding a steamer in San Pedro, California, for the trip to Catalina Island, and watching four men, complete with fat cigars, come onto the boat, go into the lounge and sit down to a game of gin rummy which continued throughout the trip and, I assume, throughout their two-week vacation. This pursuit of the same activities in changing surroundings is usually a tedious undertaking and one that is recommended only by the travel agencies.

One's life, it seems to me, is mainly enriched by engaging it within its surroundings and not by the distinctly trying activity of packing and unpacking across the world, plodding through those seemingly inexhaustible cathedrals.

A person taking a vacation during which he lives simply, rigorously, and with a complete change of habits, will find on his return to city life that he enjoys the office, the smog, and the routine. And even the conversation of fellow workers he has known for years, if not exactly replete with captivating humor and wit, will at least seem quite interesting.

It seems to me that the mistake so many of us make is that of looking for fun during a holiday when the real trick is to use a vacation to make the rest of the year fun.

I remained with my Argentine tobacco company for the record period of three years. My association with the firm came to an end in a rather odd manner.

The manager of the company became engaged to be married to the daughter of an important Argentine industrialist, who gave a small celebration dinner party at his home to which I was invited. I was to pick up a friend of mine, also a member of the company, and take him to the house as he did not know the address. When I arrived at my friend's apartment with only ten minutes to spare, I found that he had not even begun to dress. He seemed reluctant to make haste and get ready, and convinced me that I was unduly concerned about the need for punctuality since I was, after all, in a Latin country.

It was a most inaccurate and disastrous assessment of the situation, for when we finally arrived at the house—one hour late—we found that the guests numbered thirteen without us, and that they had, due to the usual superstition, been unable to sit down to dinner. The manager interpreted our belated arrival as a personal insult and refused to condone it. He held me fully responsible and succeeded in having me thrown out of the company.

I took a train across the Andes and got myself a job with a tobacco company in Valparaiso.

I was rather sad about leaving the Argentine; I had acquired a certain affection for the country. I had engaged in a lot of youthful high jinks there, such as swimming in a dinner jacket across the lake in the Parque Belgrano—or was it the Parque Palermo—I forget which, and keeping a pet ostrich in my apartment.

I missed the strange way of life that was in vogue there at the time—a way of life which embraced the nocturnal custom of locking up all the decent women behind barred windows so that the only women one saw in the street at nighttime were prostitutes.

Prostitution was legal in the Argentine in those days. There was a regularly inspected government-run brothel in every block. The prevailing atmosphere in these brothels was indistinguishable from that of a dentist's office.

The waiting rooms were furnished in a style that contrasted strongly with the concupiscent attitude of their users. There would be a central table covered with magazines of the same vintage as that favored by the medical and dental professions, a number of chairs with their backs to the wall on which sat the sober-faced customers, perusing magazines with an air of preoccupied detachment which gave the impression that their visit was anything but hedonistic. The girls were hard working and efficient, and in some cases not unattractive.

Each brothel would have one bedroom on either side of

the waiting room. While the girl was occupied with one customer in one bedroom, the other bed would be made up and fresh towels put in the room.

His brief moment of nirvana over, the customer would take his leave, the girl would walk into the waiting room, and at her "Next please" another customer would put down his magazine and disappear into the other bedroom.

Sometimes a customer, perhaps a swarthy, mustachioed gaucho in from the pampas, perhaps a bespectacled accountant from the city, would become so interested in the magazine he was reading that he would pass up his turn until later. Sometimes he would take the magazine into the bedroom with him. The whole thing was run on a sort of assembly line basis.

It is small wonder that the white slave traffic was so active in those days. The turnover in girls must have approximated the figures quoted by General Motors for Chevrolet.

Most of all I missed the music of the country—the wailing, plaintive tones of the *bandoneon,* a large squeeze-box, which for some reason has not been played very much in any other country.

It has been a source of regret to me that Argentine tango music has not achieved the popularity enjoyed by Cuban dance music: there is nothing more satisfying than the sound produced by an *orquesta típica,* which consists of two violins, two bandoneones, a piano and double bass. I have been told that the reason for its lack of popularity in places other than the Argentine is that the dance is too difficult for people to become proficient in. I can add to this that the dance is also not interesting. Yet I find the music more moving than any I have ever listened to.

My new job in Chile was sales promotion of the company's brands, an extension of the activities I had been engaged in in the Argentine.

I was sent to the north of Chile to study the local situation and make suggestions regarding methods of improving the company's penetration of the market. I took a train to Antofagasta and proceeded from there by car to reconnoiter the northern provinces of Chile. It would not be an exaggeration to say that the whole of the north of Chile, at that time, was one vast nitrate mining camp. There were a number of nitrate *oficinas* owned by various companies, which consisted of plant, machinery, and nitrate extracting and refining equipment, and housing for the personnel. Each of these *oficinas* had its own small theatre where amateur theatrical activities were engaged in, and its own general store, where everything including cigarettes were sold to the employees.

The competition was solidly entrenched and very few of the *oficinas* carried our brands.

I conceived the idea of putting on a little show at each of these theatres. Instead of making a normal charge for admission, anyone who showed a package of one of our brands of cigarettes to the ushers would be allowed to enter. In addition to this, I would have the box office decked out as a cigarette-vending kiosk. I suggested this idea to the company and they approved of it enthusiastically and gave me the green light to go ahead. I then hired two guitarists and a broken-down conjuror, which was all the budget would stand. I put together a show with these men and opened at one of the nitrate *oficinas,* while making advance bookings with the rest.

It was my first—and so far only—experience as a theatrical producer and director and I must say I quite enjoyed it, although the project as a whole had no success whatsoever. It did not serve to increase the demand for our products and I was recalled in disgrace to Valparaiso. I can sympathize with the anguish advertising men on Madison Avenue who use show business to promote sales via TV must have to endure from the manufacturers who employ them and cannot, for one moment, allow themselves to accept the idea that perhaps the customer just does not like their products.

Be that as it may my company decided to give me another chance and sent me to the south of Chile to see what I could dig up there.

The conditions in the south were vastly different from those I had but recently left behind me.

Instead of a nitrate desert with oases, I found myself in lush green country which was mostly given up to farming, and the problem was how to communicate with the farmers and break their long-standing smoking habits. The farmers would come to town only occasionally to get supplies and then go back to their farms, where they would be out of reach of any normal advertising media.

I conceived the idea of flying over the country and dropping small parachutes with samples of our brands attached to them together with leaflets addressed to the farmers, inviting them to test and enjoy the cigarettes that would fall providentially into their hands.

I suggested this to the company and obtained their approval.

There was a small military air base near Temuco, which was my base of operations, where they had about three or four ancient World War One Bristol fighters. These were the only airplanes in the whole of the south of Chile.

I made an arrangement with the base commander whereby, for a certain consideration in cash, he would remove the machine gun from the machine gun cockpit in which I would fly standing up, the parachute packages I had designed for the purpose packed around me. I then hired a number of women to make small, multicolored parachutes of tissue paper, which were designed in such a way that they would unravel automatically when packed in boxes of fifty—the boxes being designed to explode at an altitude of about three hundred feet, and thus to create a kaleidoscopic effect in the sky. With every ten boxes I had one large parachute supporting a gold watch as a sort of premium for the lucky finder.

Two days prior to the date set for the flight I dispatched a street orator whom I had hired for this purpose as a sort of advance emissary, to go from village to village, parking his car at street corners and making rabble-rousing orations to the effect that in a couple of days an airplane would fly over and drop gold watches and cigarettes, and that these were presents from the company. At that time very few people in this area had ever seen an airplane and this apparition in itself was to be an important event.

On the day of the flight everything worked according to plan until we flew over some mountainous territory where the air became extremely turbulent and the plane began to bump up and down in rather alarming fashion. I had by now made a number of successful parachute drops and had distributed perhaps half my load, but since I was not in any way attached to the plane, there were times when I found myself poised in mid-air above it, with nothing to cling to except a box containing cigarettes and tissue paper. Next moment I would be plummeted back into the cockpit with a force equivalent to several G's, which left me wondering why I did not go straight on through the bottom of the plane and out the other side. It is a tribute to the workmanship of The Bristol Bi-Plane Company that this particular plane was constructed in such a manner as to preserve me from such a catastrophe. It is also fortunate that the plane was ambling along so slowly that the air blast was insufficient to affect my involuntary jack-in-the-box activities.

Another unforeseen problem now began to claim my attention, I was becoming airsick. It is one thing to be sick in a paper bag when comfortably strapped into the seat of a modern air liner. It is quite another to be sick in mid-air. In desperation I used my glove—a purpose for which it was not primarily designed and for which it was also of somewhat insufficient capacity.

However, I successfully hid my shame from the pilot, who was sitting in front and could not see what was going on behind him.

When we finally landed at the base, I managed to achieve, still no doubt rather green in the face, something of the casual manner I felt the occasion called for.

Upon my return to the office I sat down to wait for the news that would begin to trickle through regarding the success or failure of my mission.

The first news was rather alarming. Two cases of knifing were reported by men disputing claims to the rightful ownership of gold watches that had fallen into their immediate vicinity.

By and large, the campaign stirred up a great deal of interest, and in this regard was an unqualified success. But the most important reaction came from a totally unexpected quarter.

The press of the capital city of Santiago took the matter up and banner headlines referring to the advent of modern advertising methods in Chile gave us about ten days' worth of free publicity of a kind that could not have been purchased.

I was a success and the company was pleased with me.

My success was short-lived, however. I had decided to celebrate this happy turn of events in the manner prescribed by mankind since the dawn of history—namely by inbibing an excessive amount of intoxicating liquor, or in other words getting swacked.

It was in a highly inebriated state and rather late at night that I decided to go home. I had been living for some time in a chalet on the outskirts of town as the house guest of a very charming widow, who was engaged to be married to a lawyer in Temuco.

I would have been very happy with this woman but for the nocturnal visits of her fiancé, who would remonstrate with her by banging on the shutters of our bedroom window and shouting what I felt to be totally irrelevant accusations of infidelity. He took a thoroughly middle-class attitude toward the hospitality his fiancée was showing to me. I found it extremely irksome to be awakened in the middle of the night by loud bangings on the window shutters, but the villa was more comfortable than the hotel and so I put up with it.

On the night of my triumph, however, I did not feel disposed to pursue this craven attitude, and in response to our nocturnal visitor's knocking I threw the window open wide and faced him in defiance, revolver in hand. He must have been at least as drunk, if not drunker, than I. He promptly challenged me to a duel, and I just as promptly accepted.

I climbed out of the window and dropped to the ground. I could not see him because it was pitch dark outside, but our bodies touched. We maneuvered ourselves into a back-to-back position. "Ten paces," he said. "All right," I answered, and we started to stagger away from one another. I had the advantage. I was barefoot. I could hear the crunch of his shoes on the gravel path. I turned and pressed my trigger in the direction of the last crunch. I stood my ground but there was no answering shot. I walked back in his direction and stumbled over him as he lay on the ground. I picked him up, fireman's-lift style, and carried him into the house. He was all right. The bullet had entered his neck but he wasn't bleeding much. Later they told me that if it had been a fraction of an inch to the left he would have died. As it was he was perfectly all right four days later. The bullet had turned on entering his neck and they took it out of his back. It had severed some ligaments or what-not that caused him to have a slight limp afterwards, but apart from that he was as right as rain.

I have not owned a gun since then and never will. I can never look back upon that night without a cold shiver running down my spine. It was a hairsbreadth escape for both of us.

Somebody in the house, in trying to get hold of a doctor, had described the situation too fully over the telephone and the operator had called the police. I was carted off to jail and locked up in a cell with two other men and a boy. The two men were there for forgery. The boy was awaiting trial on a charge of stealing a piece of cheese. He had been awaiting trial for eighteen months. The authorities had obviously forgotten all about him.

He had developed a very high degree of skill at a pastime which he had invented, which was to make a lasso out of twine which he would use to catch rats. By placing a piece of cheese at a distance of about six inches from a rathole, he would set the noose around the edge and wait for the rat to poke his nose out, at which time he would give a quick jerk on the twine, and nine times out of ten would catch the rat.

For all I know he may still be awaiting trial, and for all I know he may be doomed to spend the rest of his life catching rats.

I was more fortunate than he. I did not remain in prison for more than a few hours before wind of my situation reached the company. They sent a man down to do whatever was necessary to set me free. When I say they set me free—I mean they set me free. I was not only thrown out of the company, I was thrown out of South America.

CHAPTER 4

U PON MY RETURN IN DISGRACE from
South America I found it very difficult to get a job, although
eventually, through a friend of mine, I succeeded.

I became an account executive in L.I.N.T.A.S., the advertising branch of the Lever Brothers combine in London.

My duties consisted in trying to interpret the advertising
needs of our various clients and supplying those needs
through the resources of the company.

I worked in an office with three other men who took their
work so seriously that I could not resist the temptation to
dictate my requisitions in a facetious manner. I was far more
concerned in getting laughs out of them than in watching
over the interests of my clients. In the course of time this
fact was brought to the attention of my superiors and not
long afterwards I was to have an experience with which, by
now, I had become thoroughly familiar. I was unceremoni-
ously thrown out of the company.

This episode is only worth mentioning because in the office next to mine there was a beautiful redhead who was in charge of the Market Research and Information department. This girl—to whom my clients owed the fact that however else I may have failed them, I never failed to supply them with adequate market-research-and-information—was ardently interested in amateur theatricals and persuaded me to join her group one evening and read a part in a show they were intent on producing. I read the part, I like to think, to everyone's satisfaction. Yet I had not at this time the faintest idea that I would ever become an actor. I let the matter drop for want of interest. However, my interest in market research and information continued unabated, and I never lacked for excuses to wander into the office of that gorgeous redhead, where I would feast my eyes on her and enjoy her brilliant conversation. Her name was Greer Garson.

During the humiliatingly short period Lever Brothers availed themselves of my services I had been taking singing lessons from my Uncle Sacha, and by the time the manager of L.I.N.T.A.S. informed me in a manner I thought unnecessarily impolite that the company had decided to dispense with my services, I had developed a resonant bass-baritone voice.

One night at a party I was singing and playing the piano when a producer offered me a job in a revue which he was staging. I promptly accepted and have never looked forward since.

I was so bad in the revue that they finally threw me out. I then began working part-time on the B.B.C., which gave me some training, particularly in how to read lines.

From radio I went into a play called *King's Ransom* with Dennis King and Jeanne Aubert. I sang a song and played the guitar in the prison scene, but the play was not a success and closed before the director really had a chance to throw me out. I did some night club work for a while and then went into Noël Coward's *Conversation Piece* as Noël's understudy. I went to Broadway with the play and, on my return, was given the leading part opposite Edna Best in a play called *Further Outlook*.

We went on the road for a few weeks to give the production the usual tryout in the provinces. Various cuts and changes were made before the show opened in London. I was one of them.

My first appearance on the screen was as one of the gods in *The Man Who Could Work Miracles*. The part called for me to ride half-naked and shiny with grease, at four o'clock in the morning during one of England's coldest winters, on a horse which was also coated with grease. Torin Thatcher and Ivan Brandt were the other two greasy gods. Though I have never fancied myself as a horseman, I was the only one of the three that didn't fall off. In this regard at least I was already a successful film actor.

My second film was *Strange Cargo* and the third *Dishonor Bright* with Tom Walls, both made for British and Dominion Films, a company which had undertaken the not inconsiderable risk of placing me under contract. It was a promising start in the business although it wasn't long before the British and Dominion studio was reduced to ashes in a disastrous fire that providentially consumed everything except my contract.

Having nothing to do, I went to Hollywood, where 20th Century-Fox bought my slightly scorched contract and put me into *Lloyds of London* with Tyrone Power. I had had since the beginning a profound sense of unreality about my newly acquired profession which the atmosphere of Hollywood did nothing to dispel. I never really thought I would make the grade. And let's face it, I haven't.

I would say that I am about three-quarters of the way,

and this is about as far as I can get. It is far enough. It is possible that if I had started ten years earlier I might have made it all the way to the top, but acting is a profession for the young, and unless you make a solid mark when you are young, you're better off in character work. On the other hand, if you have once made your mark as a young man, then no matter what your age becomes, you are still perpetually young in the mind of your audience. Your only problem then is that of having to have your face lifted every once in a while.

When I began my career in films I found it rather frustrating not to be cast in romantic parts, since it seemed to me that I was just as handsome, dashing, and heroic as any of my contemporaries. But I soon became adjusted to the idea that I would always be cast as the villain and I have found many compensations for this state of affairs.

Incidentally, producers run into a peculiar problem when they develop the part of the villain in a script. It is the problem of giving him a suitable profession. If they make the villain a salesman, for example, thousands of outraged salesmen write in after the picture is released and bitterly protest. They maintain that salesmen are not mean. This is of course a debatable point. However, producers who have their eyes fixed on box office receipts like to see if they can please everyone.

To play it safe, a producer for whom I once worked decided to make me a professional reindeer milker, because he figured that there would be only two people in the whole of the U.S. who would have legitimate cause for complaint.

I am, at the present writing, engaged in the portrayal of the meanest man in all of old Jerusalem, which is about as mean as you can get. I am quite happy in the part and would not wish it to be softened in any way.

I made a much better adjustment in this sort of thing

than did our poor late-lamented Laird Cregar, an actor of great talent, who was virtually assassinated by Hollywood.

Since Laird's physique was rather too robust, his eyes rather curiously slanted and his features inconsistent with the general mold of the fashionable leading man, he was invariably cast as a fiend. In the preamble of every script there is a description of the leading characters.

In the case of Laird's roles the description would always be that of a subhuman monster. Time and time again, after reading the preamble in the script of a picture he was about to do, Laird would go into the make-up department and ask the chief make-up man what fantastic distortions of his face would be required for the part.

The make-up man would invariably answer, "We want you just as you are, Mr. Cregar."

The picture which expedited his demise was *Hangover Square,* in which he was a mad pianist, arsonist, rapist and murderer. He himself had induced the company to buy the book, which was about a rather gentle young man with a few psychological problems.

The change wrought in the story by the studio was too much for him and he refused to do the part. The studio, in accordance with its policy at the time, brought pressure to bear upon him and he finally succumbed. But a tragic resolve was born in Laird's mind to make himself over into a beautiful man who would never again be cast as a fiend.

He confessed this to me on the first day of shooting. He told me he was going to have an operation on his eyes and make various other changes. And that above all he was going to reduce until he became as slender as a sapling.

Soon after the picture was completed Laird Cregar entered a hospital where he literally dieted away his life.

Actors are oddly compounded of fact and fantasy. They are spell-binders who are bound by their own spells.

Sometimes this curious sorcery produces a second man, a sort of sorcerer's apprentice, or marionette, who leads a separate, almost uncontrolled life of his own, and the actor finds himself watching with great astonishment as he is identified as "The Man you love to hate" or "The World's Sweetheart" or "The stingiest man on earth," "The Blonde Bombshell" or "The First Lady of the Screen"—although this last has been regarded as an unethical short cut in the more austere circles, since it was admitted to be only a matter of wearing white gloves.

Sometimes this marionette or mask is so intoxicatingly beautiful that the wearer becomes reluctant to reveal his less enlivening aspects to the public, and retires inviolate, securely carapaced from the world by his mask.

Sometimes he becomes indistinguishable from the parts he plays, as in the case of the late Douglas Fairbanks, who led his life in a state of such uncontained euphoria, glamour and action as to make his films pale in comparison.

More often the really good actors and actresses are at their best acting. As they spend most of the twenty-four hours at their daily disposal acting, this does not in general detract from their charm.

They are apt not to be particularly practical, because although they *want* money, they *need* applause. They may want a wife but need an audience. A lot of times they want an opinion but need the dialogue.

CHAPTER 5

'Tis ten to one this play can never please
All that are here: some come to take their ease,
And sleep an act or two; but those, we fear,
W'have frighted with our trumpets; so, 'tis clear,
Abus'd extremely, and to cry, 'That's witty!'
Which we have not done neither: that, I fear,
All the expected good w'are like to hear
For this play at this time, is only in
The merciful construction of good women;
For such a one we show'd 'em: if they smile,
And say 'twill do, I know, within a while
All the best men are ours; for 'tis ill hap
If they hold when their ladies bid 'em clap.
                    —W. Shakespeare (1612–1613)

The play's the thing.
                    —W. Shakespeare (1600–1601)

Bring on the dancing girls.
                    —G. Sanders (1906–   )

IF ONE EXAMINES THE MOTIVES that prompt people to go to the theatre, it is surprising that actors manage to draw emotional nourishment from applause.

Probably no university has yet been endowed with adequate funds to launch an investigation into this subject, consequently it would be difficult to reduce it to adequate codification.

However, one is aware that there are men who take girls to the theatre purely as a preliminary to the more serious business of getting them to listen to reason afterwards.

When a couple belonging to this category applauds, the girl, fully conscious of her escort's interest, will delicately clap her perfumed hands in a manner calculated to inflame his desire, having taken her cue from the people who are actually watching the play and know what's going on on the stage. Meanwhile the man will applaud in a manner that he feels will demonstrate a fine balance between hairy-chested virility and sensitive intellectuality.

He will laugh uproariously whenever laughs are called for by the action of the play, thereby impressing his companion that he isn't missing a thing, and every once in a while he will startle the actors by giving a horse laugh where none is called for in order to prove that he is right on the ball, that no innuendo, no implication, is too subtle to slip past him unobserved.

Everything he does will be done out of consideration for

the effect he hopes it will have upon his intended victim.

This is the same man who goes to concerts and begins to applaud with great confidence in between the movements of a concerto, and freezes the rest of the audience into stunned embarrassment.

He is not always an American.

Then there is the businessman who takes his wife to the theatre in order to exhibit the jewelry he has been buying her. Nothing else can consolidate his standing in the community as effectively as his presence in the theatre with a bejeweled wife at his side. Such a man is understandably tired in the evening after a hard day at the office. Consequently one can expect him to be awake only during the overture. He can be relied upon to applaud in the right places however, even though he remains asleep while he does so. A conditioned reflex stimulated by a dig in the ribs from his socially ambitious, behavior-conscious wife will invariably produce the required reaction from him.

To what degree actors can warm to such applause is hard for me to say, but my guess is that they bow to it with the same quality of gratitude one would think they'd reserve for that of the wide-awake enthusiast.

Then there is the man who has a pet theory that there is nothing like an evening at the theatre to cure a chest cold. With leonine roars his coughing spells burst out triumphantly to shatter the painstakingly created moments of stillness that are the quintessence of the performer's art.

There is of course the very social couple who applaud inaudibly, it being rather vulgar actually to make a noise. Their purpose in going to the theatre is to acquire a point of view about the play which they use to advantage in the really serious business of their lives—the small talk at dinner parties.

There are those whose applause stems from a grim determination to enjoy whatever play they see merely because they have spent their hard-earned money for the tickets.

There are many who applaud only because they don't want people sitting next to them, even though they may be perfect strangers, to think that they don't know the form.

Lastly there is the type of applause that is given grudgingly, as a form of largesse, a condescending, sneering, yawn-accompanied, insufferably patronizing applause. It is the kind of applause that I give.

But let us consider the situation on the stage itself. The leading lady is home in bed with a cold. Her understudy is upstaging the leading man and not picking up her cues. The leading man is in a foul temper because he feels that his own laryngitis is just as severe as the leading lady's yet he alone has had the guts to show up at the theatre and demonstrate his selflessness, his devotion to duty, and his incomparable virtuosity.

After all, the show must go on. Some money-mad producer said that in the year 400 B.C. and it has stuck solid ever since.

The leading man is not only in a temper on account of his laryngitis and of having to play opposite an understudy, he is also no longer young and is having difficulty in remembering his lines—a difficulty that is not made any easier by the man who keeps coughing, or by the socialite in the front row who keeps turning her head to look through opera glasses at someone in a box.

But if we consider the relationship between the now apoplectic actor and the man who has just smothered one of his best lines with a horse laugh while successfully groping his girl friend, then I must say that the ritual of the theatre would seem to be among the strangest of tribal customs.

Rex Harrison told me that during the run of *My Fair Lady* they would often have a week booked solid by theatre parties consisting of groups who would come from some hick town and find the play utterly incomprehensible.

The perfectionist on the stage tends to examine more and more minutely, as with a microscope whose power continually increases, what he feels to be areas in which he believes he can improve his performance of a given part. If the audience does not respond in the expected manner, he is forced into an agonizing reappraisal of his artistic concepts.

A really good evening in the theatre, an evening when the actor and his audience are in perfect rapport, is therefore mathematically improbable. I'm sure that Lloyd's of London would gladly issue an insurance policy against such an eventuality at a modest premium. Consequently the actor who strives for the ultimate is by and large engaged in a futile quest for the end of the rainbow. Moreover, he is no better off if he happens to be among the few who find it. These few, once the moment is past, are doomed to a "remember when" situation.

Of course, this is just my private point of view, and there are probably not many actors who would agree with me, *quot homines tot sententiae.*

For myself, I am content with mediocrity and I defy any producer to send me a good script. Since I confine my activities to the movies, the fructification of such an eventuality is extremely unlikely.

In the movies we do not have to cope with any of the problems mentioned earlier. No ambitious understudy can ever hope to go on in our place. We luxuriate in the knowledge that his talents will never be discovered.

In movie-making the perfectionists among us are invariably at a disadvantage because scenes are shot before we have time to get interested in them. This is done partly for reasons of economy, and partly because the scenes are not interesting anyway.

We have no problem with audience response because our only audience is the director who is paid to tell us that we are great.

There are a few directors who make a fine show of having several takes of a given shot and, with a tortured intellectual look, either shout or whisper a lot of complicated instructions between each take regarding the manner in which they feel we can improve the scene, but the results they achieve are not better than those obtained by the directors who give no instructions of any kind. They are after all only photographing rehearsals which never have time to become scenes.

But since the average audience is incapable of distinguishing between the first reading of a competent actor and what his highly polished performance would be if he worked on it for months, the arrangement seems to me to be quite satisfactory. Anyway, in making a film the actor is always so far removed from his potential that his frustrations are of a lower order of magnitude.

The average audience is also incapable of distinguishing between a good actor and a good part. The actor gets the credit every time when more often than not the credit should go to the writer.

Yet I for one have no quarrel with such a state of affairs. Much as I admire the writers who provide us with our material, I think they should be kept in their place. Shakespeare may have been right when he said "The play's the thing," but let us not underrate the great performers. No ordinary mortals are they, but beings who have the God-given power to bind us in their magic spells not only for an evening, but for a lifetime of enchanted memories.

CHAPTER 6

O F ALL ROADS TO PUBLIC ACCLAIM in show business the hardest of all, and the one that seems to many the easiest, is that of a singer.

There is no more unreliable instrument than the human voice.

You can have a temperature of 102, a bad cold, laryngitis and a hangover and still operate satisfactorily with a piano, violin, guitar or trombone. As an actor you can give a rather husky, febrile performance that many will find more interesting than what you do when you are well. But if it is the tonal beauty of your singing voice that you are selling, watch out. Your voice will reflect your physical condition more accurately to your own ear than any or all of the diagnostic devices at the disposal of the medical profession.

After years of training and study, singers develop such a keen appreciation of the subtle fluctuations in tonal quality their voices are capable of undergoing even during the course of a single day that their lives become a veritable torment of uncertainty.

During the season at Milan the principal tenors sleep on their sides like prize fighters in training for a championship, so as not to be weakened by nocturnal emissions; while during the day they speak only in whispers, their throats covered up with mufflers, in constant dread of the ever present danger of laryngitis.

A singer who wishes to remain on top of the heap, or even on a competitive basis with those who are somewhere near the top, has no other life than the cultivation of his voice. To keep it in shape he must make sacrifices no one in any other walk of life would consider for a moment. He must cease to be a human being and become a musical instrument from head to toe. He must devote twenty-three hours a day to preparing for the one hour during which he will come to life and sing.

Caruso used to say that if he went one whole day without vocalizing he would notice the difference in his voice. After two days his wife would notice it, and after three the public would.

If physical exercise is taken during the day it will lighten the voice and elevate its over-all range by as much as one whole tone. But if the singer lies in bed all day long, his voice will be deep and full.

Caruso made use of this phenomenon and would suit his activities during the day to the part he happened to be singing at night. If he was scheduled to sing a lyric role he would take exercise, if a dramatic one he would lie in bed.

The better the singer the greater his inner torment. The keener his musical sense the greater the anguish he will suffer due to the insecurity he will feel as he nods to the conductor, faces his audience, opens his mouth, takes in his first deep breath, clasps his hands and propels the air through his vocal cords, hoping to God that the sound he produces bears some resemblance to the right musical tone.

It is one of the bitter ironies of fate that singers by and large are not gifted with a very keen sense of pitch. There are very few who can read music and fewer still who have what is known as "perfect" pitch.

There will always be musicians in the orchestra accompanying a singer who are gifted with perfect pitch even though they do not need it for the type of instrument they play, whereas the singer who needs it desperately will more than likely be gifted with a tin ear.

To tantalize him even more, the singer will constantly run into nonprofessionals with better potential organs than his. Men and women who just do not happen to be interested in developing their voices.

As he deposits his painfully earned loot at the bank he will detect the resonant baritone of the cashier. Mornings will bring him into contact with the dramatic tenor of the milkman. Ah, he thinks, what I could do with such a voice! What a Cavaradossi I would make! Then he hears the sonorous basso profundo of the gardener talking to the lyric soprano of the cook and he sees himself wowing audiences at the Met as the High Priest in Aida.

For many years the principal tenor at the Mariinsky Theatre in St. Petersburg was a man whose voice was cultivated rather than natural and was of a rather poor quality with very little reserve strength. Yet he was a man of such highly developed histrionic skill and musical talent that he was able to give renditions of arias and produce acting performances of such matchless polish that the quality of his voice was an insignificant detail in the over-all spell he succeeded in weaving around his public.

In the course of time his top notes began to crack and the

public for the first time became aware of his voice. He lost his popularity overnight and forthwith proceeded to drink himself to death.

Even at the height of his fame his life must have been a hell of torment. How wise is the cashier, the milkman and the gardener to let sleeping dogs lie.

There are, of course, a few magic voices that find their way into the right physical envelopes, but their owners then have so much success that they develop personality disturbances curable only by psychiatry or alcohol.

My first engagement as a professional singer was in the London Revue *Ballyhoo*. I had to sing a song from one of the boxes situated high up at the back of the theatre. The distance from the orchestra to my ear was just too great for my sense of pitch. The result was that I sang the whole song off-key every night to long-suffering audiences and a management less willing to suffer that soon lost patience and threw me out of the show.

Yet there is nothing I could have done other than have a man up in the box with a tuning fork and this I could not afford.

Subsequent appearances I have made as a singer were less painful to the audience though hardly any more successful. Perhaps the high spot of my singing career was an appearance I made on the Tallulah Bankhead radio show some years ago when I sang the aria "Il lacerato spiritu" from the opera *Simon Boccanegra* accompanied by a fifty-piece orchestra conducted by Meredith Willson: I sang it in tune, my voice was in perfect shape and my rendition, according to my teacher, had exactly the right emotional shadings.

When I came to the end of the aria and bowed low to the audience, there followed that moment of stunned silence before the applause that is so dear to every performer.

In my case, however, the moment lasted so long that

Tallulah had to come to my rescue with a few well-chosen ad libs.

However, on the whole, I have fared much better than those unfortunate singers who do not possess the faculty of being able to exercise critical judgment upon themselves. The rather portly females, for example, who cannot wait to be asked to sing at a party but get up and do so at the drop of a hat to the frozen embarrassment of the unfortunate guests.

The only real fun to be had out of singing is in learning to sing. The development of the motor muscles of the vocal cords and the consequent production of resonant tones give the student a sort of horticultural satisfaction. Singing teachers themselves are such fabulous characters with their *bel-canto* double talk and their unshakable faith in the supremacy of their systems that their lessons have a definite therapeutic value comparable to, if not surpassing, that of the analyst's couch. Unless you desperately need the money it is really a mistake to put the result of their teaching to the test on the concert platform. It is wiser to go on learning and improving and to walk through life with the inner conviction, bolstered by the teachers' assurances, that if one ever did put one's vocal powers to the test it would cause a revolution at the Scala Milan.

Fortified and sustained in such a schizophrenic cloud of unreality one can enjoy to the full the satisfactions of an ever burgeoning art without having to forego the pleasures of smoking and drinking, or restrict that other activity which moralists call overrated but about which you and I know better.

For always remember that if you are a professional there can be no "Last lay for the minstrel."

CHAPTER 7

SHORTLY AFTER MY ARRIVAL in Holly-
wood, before my features had become irrevocably and irrepa-
rably molded into the expression of elegant villainy which
I am assured I possess today, I had my opportunity to become
a romantic star. Louis B. Mayer, in what was possibly one
of his less enlightened moments, had come to the conclusion
that he could turn me into a star who would make the
world's heart, tired as it was, throb a little faster.

He had achieved this much for Lassie and, I imagine, was
now disposed to take on something more difficult, namely—
me. Though I can state without undue conceit that I have
more sex-appeal than Lassie, I doubt whether I would have
been as rewarding a proposition for Louis B. For one thing,
I suspect I am not as good an actor as Lassie and furthermore
I am a man who is more likely to suffer from palpitations
than to give them to others. Nonetheless, Mayer was of the

opinion that I was star material and he invited me to lunch to discuss the possibility of my leaving 20th Century-Fox and joining Metro-Goldwyn-Mayer.

It is an indication of how much he had overestimated my ambitiousness and my malleability that I never even turned up for the lunch. I was otherwise engaged at the time building a telescope in my back garden and being, by vocation, a dilettante, this interested me far more than the golden future which Mr. Mayer was going to offer me on a silver platter.

I got a certain amount of fun out of the telescope, studying the planets, but it was of absolutely no use for studying bathing belles or disrobing ladies as it had an inverted image. I eventually sold the telescope to Universal International for $500, and they used it—and me—in the film *Uncle Harry*.

Perhaps my curious indifference to success will be more understandable if I explain that the driving force of my life has always been laziness; to practice this, in reasonable comfort, I have even been prepared, from time to time, to work. I think I knew instinctively that being a romantic star would demand of me, in terms of time and effort, more than I was inclined to give. I was only interested in getting to the top the easy way, and if I couldn't get to the top the easy way, I would settle for getting *some* of the way the easy way.

I had become a Hollywood actor earning a handsome salary without exerting myself unduly; and if Fate had been disposed to make me a heartthrob, a pin-up, a Great Lover, I would have acquiesced with my normal graciousness. But I wasn't going to indulge in any Promethean struggle in order to achieve this goal. Quite honestly I didn't care all that much.

Perhaps I did make a mistake in not accepting Mayer's invitation, but looking back on this crucial moment in my career I can only feel regret at having missed what would undoubtedly have been an excellent lunch. Had I become a big-time romantic star I might now be a good deal richer than I am; on the other hand it is quite conceivable I would no longer be around, professionally speaking: the mortality rate among stars is extremely high, whereas a good character actor is almost indestructible. Even with one foot in the grave it is possible for such an actor to go on earning a good living, since there seem to be a large number of parts written which require the actor to look half dead: and in fact these circumstances may lend a verisimilitude to his performance which his acting never could.

My career having taken the turn it did, I am, at the age of fifty-three, in the fortunate position of not having to worry that I look every day of fifty-four. When a new line makes its debut on my face I can take it.

When I begin to suffer from arthritis I shall be able to exploit my misfortune to the full, extracting every last ounce of sympathy and help from friends and relatives, whereas if I had been a romantic star I would clearly have been obliged to keep my arthritis to myself and suffer it in silence and secrecy. Indeed I should have had to prove to the world how athletic I still was, a task which I would have found un-bearably onerous even at the unarthritic age of seventeen.

When I try to discover what is the indispensable quality, one which I obviously lack, that is necessary to become a star I come to the conclusion that it is the *desire* to be a star. Even those who profess most strenuously that they loathe all the vulgar curiosity which they attract would, I am sure, be perfectly miserable without it. This is where I differ from them. It is generally recognized that the people who write fan letters to film stars or hysterically seek to divest their favorite performer of some article of his clothing belong to the lunatic fringe, and, speaking for myself, I am content to remain unpopular with the lunatic fringe. If all this sounds rather like sour grapes that is because it is sour grapes—to some extent at any rate. There are moments when I see the story of my career, which might be entitled The Man Who Didn't Come to Lunch, as a full-scale tragedy. Usually I take this view when I read about other actors receiving $2,000,000 for one film. At such moments I tend to consider that $2,000,000 is a reasonable amount of hush money for keeping one's arthritis secret.

The suspicion that I may possibly have missed something by not lunching with Louis B. Mayer was aroused in me again during the making of Solomon and Sheba, when I had an opportunity to observe Yul Brynner, who is, of course, a very big romantic star despite being, in at least one respect, less abundantly endowed than I.

After Tyrone Power's death, Brynner arrived in Madrid to take over the part of Solomon. Inspired no doubt by the grandeur of his role, he also brought an entourage of seven. The function of one member of this retinue appeared to consist entirely of placing already lighted cigarettes in Brynner's outstretched fingers. Another was permanently occupied in shaving his skull with an electric razor whenever the suspicion of a shadow darkened that noble head. While these services were being rendered unto him, Brynner sat in sphynxlike silence and splendor wearing black leather suits or white leather suits, of which he had half a dozen each, confected for him by the firm of Dior.

I never discovered what were the duties of the remaining five members of his staff, but they were no doubt doing work that was equally essential. I must admit that I have never felt unduly hard done by because I have had to light my own cigarettes—still, I was impressed. I came to the conclusion that Brynner is a very shrewd fellow; he has one very intense expression which he uses all the time on the screen, and one intense expression is more valuable to a film star than a dozen faces. If I have learned anything in the movie business it is that it pays to let the camera act for you. Regardless of the dramatic content of a particular scene, a close-up of the star looking intense is always highly effective. It hardly matters what comes before or after.

The important thing, for a film star, is to have an interesting face. He doesn't have to move it very much. Editing and camera work can always produce the desired illusion that an acting performance is being given.

If I seem to be biting the hand that has fed me quite adequately for nearly 25 years, that is because I have never been madly enthusiastic about film acting. As an art it is rather like roller-skating; once you know how to do it, it isn't particularly stimulating intellectually; it is not very exciting; it is hard work; and it takes up a lot of time that might be more profitably employed.

If you ask how I might employ my time more profitably I can only reply—by not acting. Not to be an actor is, I think, a most laudable ambition, and one which a lot of young people might do well to acquire. The real trouble about being an actor is that you are expected to be good. That is all right for those fanatics who wish to impress posterity, or for anyone who has the good fortune to lack the critical acumen which would tell him how bad he really is.

Being a person of the highest taste, I am continually incurring my own disapproval, since my standards are too high for my performance ever to come up to them. I expect perfection but can only provide mediocrity.

It gives me no particular satisfaction to think that actors even more mediocre than I are hailed as great artists; it merely proves what lamentable taste most people have.

I know that it is customary in an actor's autobiography to recall one's triumphs and failures with a becoming mixture of modesty and egotism; one asserts that one really gave one's best performances in the films the public failed to appreciate and one insists, not too strenuously of course, that the performance for which one is most celebrated was done after a night out with the boys and in a condition of semiconsciousness.

Having found such confessions excruciatingly dull when made by other actors, I do not propose to bore you—or, what is more to the point, myself—by falling into the same error. I can state without fear of contradiction that I am an even worse actor drunk than I am sober, that I believe in learning my lines and, whenever this is not too harrowing, speaking them. If I have occasionally given brilliant performances on the screen, this was entirely due to circumstances beyond my control. The blunt truth is that I invariably play myself. Sometimes playing myself is appropriate to the part and then I receive rave notices and even an Oscar (as I did for *All About Eve*); at other times playing myself is singularly inappropriate to the circumstances of the story and then I am quite rightly panned. Therefore the only credit I can claim for myself is that I have occasionally chosen—or been bribed into playing—the right parts.

I have not, of course, always been in a position to choose, and this sometimes produced curious situations.

One of my earliest successes was in a film called *Lancer Spy* in which I played a double role. In one of these roles, as a Nazi officer, I wore a monocle to some effect. As a result of this, when my next role came along, that of a pirate in a thing called *Slave Ship*, I was again called upon to wear a monocle. It was useless for me to protest that at the time of this particular story monocles had not yet been invented. Such pedantry made little impression on the film's producer, and I duly became history's first monocled pirate.

I was eventually allowed to dispense with monocles, but

the character I had played in *Lancer Spy* was more difficult to get rid of. For a long time I was considered the ideal actor to play sneering, arrogant, bull-necked Nazi brutes. Nobody, it seems, could enunciate the word *Shweinehund,* which constituted a large part of the dialogue in such films, quite as feelingly as I.

There was a limit to the number of Nazi roles that could be offered to me, and eventually I was allowed to do other things. But by this time I had been typed. I was definitely a nasty bit of goods. My nastiness however was of a novel kind. I was beastly but I was never coarse. I was a high-class sort of heel. If the plot required me to kill or maim anybody I always did so in a well-mannered way and if I may say so, with good taste. And I always wore a clean shirt. I was the sort of villain who was finicky about getting blood on his clothes; it wasn't so much that I cared about being found out, but I liked to look neat.

I cannot pretend that I found my career very much of a struggle or that there was a triumphal moment when I suddenly knew I had made it, which may of course be because that moment never came. To become a star overnight is both an exhilarating and an unbalancing experience; it did not happen to me. My progress was slow and steady; I grew accustomed to having a famous face. By the time I had attained the degree of notoriety that insured recognition anywhere in the world, it seemed perfectly natural. I am a drifter, and I drifted into fame.

On the whole, the advantages of being famous outweigh the drawbacks: headwaiters, hotel managers, members of the aristocracy and certain women are liable to be fascinated by a "name" and this occasionally pays off. It really has nothing to do with whether they admire you or not, they may consider you a thundering bore as an actor and an unmitigated blackguard as a person, but if you are famous the headwaiters will give you the best tables, the hotel managers will keep you the best suite, the aristocracy will invite you to their castles . . . and one or two ladies will bestow favors upon you—a flowery phrase to which I am deeply devoted, more perhaps to the phrase than the fact, which can sometimes lead to situations of absolutely ghastly embarrassment.

On one occasion after I had arrived in London I received a request for an interview from a lady purporting to be a journalist. It was immediately after a press reception which had been given for me and the lady said she wished to ask me some supplementary questions. In accordance with my usual attitude toward such requests I was beginning to frame a negative rejoinder when my producer, with whom I had been chatting, took me aside and began to explain to me the importance of preserving good relations with the press.

"But it is such a bore," I said. "And anyway they always write the same old nonsense whether you talk to them or not."

"You seem to have no regard for your employers or the hazards they assume when they employ you," said my employer. "It is vitally important to our picture that we win the wholehearted co-operation of the press. Now please stop being such a sonofabitch and ask the dame up for a drink."

Stung by this rebuke my sensitive nature could only respond by putting on what I hoped to be an expression of lamblike courtesy, and, doing as I was asked, I invited the lady to my suite.

I had not really noticed her much until she swept into my sitting room, but now I saw she was dressed entirely in a neckline which had plunged beyond recall, and an absolutely disastrous hat like a soup tureen from which she held a muffled and, as it were, sub-tureenean conversation.

She swigged down two drinks in rapid succession and seemed to be in high good humor though there were none of the "further questions" which had been mentioned earlier. In fact her conversation was finally more or less restricted to a few confidential sort of hiccups.

Then, starting on her third drink and turning her tureen carefully toward me, she finally delivered the question she had in mind.

It was not a journalistic type of question; as a matter of fact it was more of a request than a question, and more of a command than either. I gazed at her, or such areas as were not obstructed by the tureen, in the greatest consternation. The Relief of Mafeking was nothing to that which I felt when in the midst of this tricky moment the phone rang. It was of course also with indescribable satisfaction that I found on completing my conversation that she had left. This naïve illusion was soon to be shattered however and I received a very ugly jolt on strolling cheerfully into my bedroom to discover the damnable hat balanced on my bedpost —where it looked rather better actually than it had on the girl—and its owner bare as a radish all over my bed.

Inasmuch as every other actor I know has encountered a similar experience it does lead one to speculate on the great amount of time and thought given by tremulous parents to the protection of their daughters against the hazards of life in general and the aggressions of men in particular. This is the kind of situation which leads one to consider who is protecting whom and against what. To finish this indelicate story I hasten to say at once that it developed the lady was in no way connected with the press.

I say "hasten" because I am well aware of the probity of every member of the press, and considering the pious horror with which they report all the diversions from chastity of the rest of us it makes it doubly improper that any such behavior should be ascribed to one of their members, even for a few moments.

As to the denouement of my own predicament I can only repeat at the risk of being ungallant—which is a risk I will quite cheerfully take—that bestowal of favors is not all it is cracked up to be, and it took me as much time, trouble, maneuvering and psychology to get that lady out of my bed as it has ever taken, in other circumstances, to get one in! I considered suing my unprincipled producer for contributing to my moral delinquence, but he is a man of low character and was seized with such a fit of coarse laughter when I told of the results of his instructions that I decided not to risk entertaining him further. However, these experiences leave their mark and I still regard the press with cautious reserve.

Needless to say, not every male film star necessarily finds such situations embarrassing. Some consider these particular fruits of fame as no more than their due, along with other privileges like getting the best tables at restaurants.

It is just as well that there are some compensations for being an actor, for it is a life that in other respects has decided disadvantages.

In any other business, as you become more successful you work less; you acquire minions who relieve you of the more onerous tasks. The actor cannot, however famous and successful, get somebody else to act for him. He always has to do it himself. The industrialist does not have to build factories and the oil tycoon does not have to dig his own wells in the desert. And a general does not personally have to stick bayonets into his enemy. In all these walks of life it is recognized that as soon as you are really good at something you can get somebody else to do it for you.

On the other hand the film actor has to do it all himself,

he must perpetually manipulate his own body like a marionette; the better he is the bigger his parts and the more he
has to work. The successful banker can arrive at his office
at midday, dictate a few letters and then go off and play golf
all afternoon. Even Presidents of the United States seem to
be able to run affairs of state from a golf course. But the
unfortunate actor invariably has to present himself in person
before the cameras and sweat it out. He has to ride horses,
get dirty—and he has, worst of all, to get up at the crack of
dawn. This is the part of the job that I resent most bitterly.

Somewhat belatedly I have come to the conclusion that my
real vocation in life is to be idle; this is something at which
I could really shine. It seems most unfortunate that I have
not been provided either with the courage or the means to
practice it. It is one of the sad ironies of life that one has
to make money in order to spend time but waste time in
order to make money.

In the days when Hollywood was in its infancy everybody
believed in spending money. They spent it with a gleeful
abandon that only the poor can understand. They were
much more interested in the glitter than in the gold, and
as a matter of fact I think maybe they had something there.

As soon as stars became producers, their attitude to money
changed: they wanted to keep it. They acquired financial
acumen and started saving.

This of course was not true of all of them—Ty Power's
attitude for instance was different. He spent his money freely.
He had a yacht, a private airplane, and gave lavish parties.
And women, who are usually more expensive than yachts
and airplanes, found ways of spending his money when he
ran out of ideas. Ty didn't seem to mind. Perhaps he had
some premonition that he did not need to save for his old
age.

As soon as I was getting a decent salary in Hollywood, I built myself a comfortable house, put in a croquet lawn, a tennis court, and a swimming pool. I also bought a modest size yacht. It was only then that I discovered why you need to be a millionaire in order to enjoy such luxuries, not in themselves prohibitively expensive.

The trouble is that when you have a yacht you cannot go cruising in it alone; you have to invite people to accompany you which means you have to feed them and keep them supplied with drink. Since there are more people in Hollywood with yachts than without, you are constantly competing for the company of the few yachtless ones, who consequently can afford to pick and choose their hosts. Therefore you suddenly find yourself in the position of a struggling restaurateur trying to bring in the customers. You have to offer a better spread, more drink, prettier girls. You have to bribe, blackmail, seduce or torture people into coming on your boat. You can never rest. Since you are employing a crew at ridiculous cost to keep your boat clean and in good running order, you feel obliged to spend all of your weekends on it. This means that when you could be resting peacefully with a drink in your hand in your own garden, you are being tossed about on a choppy sea, desperately trying to keep your guests entertained and fed and also coping with mutinous crews who are threatening to desert you and join Errol Flynn.

That at least was my experience. How I longed for the days when I, too, was a privileged guest on other people's yachts, feted and flattered, my company sought after, the condescending recipient of my host's food, drink, girl friends and grateful thanks.

I got rid of my yacht.

Then I had to feed only the people who came to play

croquet in my garden, serve drinks to those who acquired what seemed to be an unquenchable thirst after beating the pants off me at tennis, and tidy up the mess made by those who swam in my pool.

I got rid of my house.

CHAPTER 8

I FIND IT DIFFICULT to remember all the films I have acted in, partly due to normal middle-aged amnesia and partly to a stubborn subconscious that doesn't want me to recall to mind the attendant sufferings.

According to the reference books which consider it worth while collating such trivia, I have made about seventy films. Glancing down the list, I find I made things like *Action in Arabia, Lured,* and *The Scarlet Coat.* I can only assume that I was paid handsomely for them, but I am at a complete loss as to what action there was in Arabia, or who was lured where, and why. As to the scarlet coat, did I wear it, and if not who did?

I suppose the best film I have been in was *All About Eve.* The critics and the trade loved it. It was a film of distinction: witty, sophisticated, and brilliantly written and directed. Yet despite the acclaim heaped upon it, it did not do well at the box office.

To be commercially successful, a film has to adhere to one of about three basic formulae. The most profitable and sure-fire of these has always been: boy meets girl, boy loses girl, boy gets girl back again. Within this framework, it is permissible to do all sorts of things—one can be witty, daring, original, profound, or even dull. One has a great deal of latitude. The boy for instance can be a dipsomaniac, and the girl can be a misguided member of the Ku Klux Klan, as long as they meet, part and get together again. Or the boy can be a Martian and the girl a Mormon. The permutations are infinite—it isn't even necessary for the protagonists to be Homo sapiens, as Disney has proved.

In the case of *All About Eve* there was no such appeal to basic emotions. Our film was about sophisticated, ambitious, wickedly amusing people. The audience wasn't rooting for any of us. Anne Baxter, who was the nearest thing to a heroine in our story, was an actress passionately in love with success. What she lusted after was an Oscar. When she got her Oscar in the end, this was, to the public, a poor substitute for getting a man.

The public, after all, cannot be expected to think like actresses. I played a cynical critic, and the only person who ever loves a critic is his mother and an actor who has had a good notice from him. There are not enough critics' mothers or favorably noticed actors in the world to fill the cinemas.

Bette Davis played an egomaniacal star of Broadway, a vain, aging, flamboyant, temperamental woman—she acted superbly, but how many members of the audience could, or would have cared to, identify themselves with her?

I got an Oscar for my performance in *All About Eve* which, I suppose, makes this film the high point of my career. If I sound doubtful about it, it is because Oscars—for which so many actors and actresses pine and scheme—

have affected the recipients' careers in such an adverse way as to make them view the whole thing with some apprehension as well as pride. I was grateful and flattered to get mine, but apart from making my already large ego one size larger it did absolutely nothing for me. Far worse, however, has been the experience of other actors—as for example Luise Rainer, who hit the jackpot when she got an Oscar two years running and was never heard of again. It is a curious fact that the list of actors who have gone on and on in a state of unwavering popularity without benefit of Oscars includes three of the most distinguished. Douglas Fairbanks Sr. received one after he had died, Garbo after she had retired, and Chaplin not at all.

It is generally imagined that after receiving an Academy Award one's salary shoots up. From personal experience I have to report that this is not so, and judging by the case histories of some of the winners, one is lucky still to receive any salary at all.

The truth of the matter is that while Hollywood *admires* people who win Oscars, it *employs* people who make money, and to be able to do one does not necessarily mean you can do the other.

But be that as it may, everyone wants an Oscar, and the handing out of these coveted trophies takes place at a highly emotional ceremony which makes strong men weak and turns egocentric actresses into weeping and blushing maidens. The correct procedure for winners is to disclaim all credit for their victory and to look stunned and transported with ecstatic disbelief and surprise. This is the moment when one draws to the limit on one's reservoir of histrionic skill.

The resulting performance is usually even better than that for which one has won the award. It is neither here nor there that you and your studio and your press agents have been buying space in the trade papers for months previously informing everyone, particularly the members of the Academy of Motion Picture Arts and Sciences, how much you deserve to win.

The night I got my Oscar I was accompanied to the ceremony by Zsa Zsa Gabor, to whom I was then married. The occasion for me was filled with such painful suspense that I never rose above a state of frozen stupefaction, in contrast to Zsa Zsa who was soaring and plunging between enough dizzy emotional heights and depths for both of us, first of all with delight at attending this top-flight Beano, secondly with triumph at being associated with the winning team, and thirdly with black indignation when it was tactfully explained to her that she had not won a prize herself. She was scarcely eligible by virtue of the fact that she had not as yet made any films, but this quirk of circumstance seemed irrelevant to her, and for some time afterwards she remained both hurt and insulted.

All About Eve was also notable because in it Marilyn Monroe made one of her first appearances—as my girl friend. She played a very dumb would-be actress who I was taking around. Even then she struck me as a character in search of an author and I am delighted she found Mr. Miller eventually. She was very beautiful and very inquiring and very unsure—she was somebody in a play not yet written, uncertain of her part in the over-all plot. As far as I can recall, she was humble, punctual and untemperamental. She wanted people to like her.

I thought she had a glittering future before her, but then judging by their reminiscences and statements to the press, so did everyone else: in the circumstances it is not surprising that Marilyn soon got together with the glittering future we all foresaw for her.

I lunched with her once or twice during the making of the film and found her conversation had unexpected depths.

She showed an interest in intellectual subjects which was, to say the least, disconcerting. In her presence it was hard to concentrate.

What made me sure that Marilyn would eventually make it was that she so obviously needed to be a star; in these matters needs count for more than intrinsic talent. There are many highly talented people in all walks of life who never reach the pinnacle of their profession while less talented people do. The people who do get there usually have some deep psychological need to be on top, and this will make them exert themselves beyond their natural capacities. Marilyn is said to have spent her childhood in an orphanage and with foster parents; she had been neglected and un-loved; nobody took any notice of her until at the age of fifteen she put on a sweater. Thereafter she was not lacking in tenders of affection; once a woman puts on a sweater she has as it were a joker up her sleeve. To a girl with Marilyn's background and foreground to be a film star meant to be universally loved.

Clearly it is no accident that an unloved girl from an orphanage should become the outstanding Love Symbol of her day, but part of the psychological scheme of things.

I know, in my own case, that the kind of actor I have become has been determined to a large extent by the weakness of my character. On the screen I am usually suave and cynical, cruel to women and immune to their slights and caprices. This is my mask, and it has served me faithfully for 25 years. But in reality I am a sentimentalist, especially about myself—readily moved to tears by cheap emotions and invariably the victim of woman's inhumanity to man.

That I should choose to protect my easily wounded and ultrasensitive nature by adopting my particular mask is un-derstandable. Fortunately my mask has not only protected me but provided me with a living. Perhaps the greatest fulfillment in acting is not just the satisfaction involved in the opportunity for the extrovert to exhibit himself but more the opportunity to act out that part of himself for which he has the imagination and the capacity, but not the heart or the courage.

Sometimes people are all of a piece—Rubinstein, Douglas Fairbanks Sr., Gloria Swanson, and John McCormack are some of those who showed the same assurance and exhibited the same zest and talent in life as they did in their performances on the screen and the concert platform. But they are among the exceptions.

One thinks of Danny Kaye, so warm, so free and funny on stage, and in person filled with melancholy, somber, confused and suspicious. Jack Benny, on stage stingy, egotistical and funny, in life generous, gregarious and rather solemn. Jean Harlow, the *femme fatale* of her day, in life full of apprehensions, shy and puzzled. Cary Grant, witty, sophisticated and infinitely debonair, in life a prey to theosophical charlatans, socially insecure, and inclined to isolation. Basil Rathbone, master of the curled lip and patronizing glance, but in life warm, cozy, and a pushover for a laugh. Vincent Price, another consummate villain, is an uproarious host, warmhearted and kind, and full of love for his fellow men. Charles Laughton, an unprincipled sadist on the screen and stage, in life is interested in the gentle arts, paintings, porcelain, people, and poetry. The same of course also applies to Eddie Robinson. Theda Bara, who became synonymous with women at their most lethal, led a life of exemplary tranquillity and marital probity off the screen. Unlike Joan Fontaine, whose pure profile, austere hair-do and impeccable bearing on screen are in fine contrast to a private life of considerable vitality and color.

I mention all of the foregoing examples merely in order to make it easier for you to understand that whereas on the screen I am invariably a sonofabitch, in life I am a dear, dear, boy.

CHAPTER 9

WHEN IT BECAME KNOWN that Ezio Pinza was leaving the cast of the fabulously successful Broadway production of *South Pacific* and that a replacement would be needed, I suddenly had the brilliant idea that I should be that replacement.

Throughout most of my career the public had been allowed to remain blissfully ignorant of the fact that I was a trained singer. I decided it was high time I stopped hiding my light under a bushel and revealed myself to the world in my true vocal splendor.

I immediately set about getting my voice into condition, its natural beauty having been somewhat impaired by many years of singing bawdy songs at friends' parties. The more I practiced and polished, the more convinced I became that at last I was about to fulfill my destiny; everything had been leading up to this. As yet Dick Rodgers and Oscar Hammerstein were quite oblivious of their impending good fortune and they were, as a consequence, still in a state of mournful depression, having failed not only to find any suitable replacement but even to think of one. At this opportune moment I struck. I let it be known that I might consider playing the part. What was more, I could sing. I don't think they really believed me. Anyway, I was asked to give an audition.

As I think I have indicated elsewhere, I am not the most industrious of men, but on this occasion I did make an effort. And when Oscar Hammerstein heard me, I was good. He was not prepared to commit himself straightaway. He and Dick Rodgers had been racking their brains for weeks to try to think of someone who could fill the role—they had unaccountably failed to think of me. That the perfect actor should voluntarily materialize and solve all their problems seemed too good to be true.

If my audition did not completely convince Hammerstein, it convinced me. I was the right man for the part. I was prepared to stake their reputation on it. To bring the producers round to my point of view, I made a record privately of the hit numbers from the show and sent it to them. It must have convinced them, or else they were getting desperate, for I was given the part. Contracts were drawn up, and we all signed.

Shortly after these formalities I returned to California. And suddenly I got panicky. I had signed up for 15 months. What had I let myself in for? It seemed like a jail sentence to me; I had never been in a stage production before, I was not what is known as a trouper; I did not subscribe to the sentimental and entirely fallacious notion that the show must go on. With me in it, the odds were that the show quite frequently wouldn't go on. I could not visualize myself "carrying on in defiance of doctor's orders" as good troupers are reputed to do. It was all very well saying I would do the show now when I actually wanted to, but in the course of a year one's whole life can change—one might have got married or divorced, or become a father, or a Buddhist or a vegetarian.

To guarantee in writing that 14 months from that day I would still be standing on the same stage singing the same songs and speaking the same dialogue seemed to me like an extraordinary piece of presumption. God might have alternative plans for me. How could I possibly know how I would feel and think in six months' time, let alone 14 months' time? The perennial bachelor in me who resents all ties and restrictions rebelled against such a limitation of his freedom. I felt as if I had been the victim of a shotgun wedding: I had seduced Rodgers and Hammerstein into giving me the part and now I was married to them for 15 months—without even Reno or Las Vegas by way of an escape clause.

Thereupon I developed a backache. And the fact that the doctors could find no physical cause for it did not lessen the severity of the pain. Just as I had previously been obsessed with the desire to be in the show, I was now obsessed with an even greater desire to be out of it. There was nothing for it but to write to Rodgers and Hammerstein, explain about my back, and beg to be released from my contract. Very generously they agreed to give me my freedom.

No sooner had I been freed from my commitment than the backache vanished.

It was then that I decided I ought to see a psychiatrist. I had just thrown up an opportunity I would probably never have again; for weeks I had worked and plotted and schemed to get that part in *South Pacific* and then when I had got it, I didn't want it. I was ripe for the headshrinkers.

Before I relate my ensuing adventures on various assorted couches, I want to state quite unequivocally that I am one of the sanest people I know. If I weren't, I would never have risked going to a psychiatrist.

Altogether I tried six of them before finding one which suited me.

The first one had an office in a skyscraper in New York. He charged $50 an hour and he saw me every day for one hour. His office looked just like any lawyer's office except that it had a couch in it. Perhaps what sold me on the idea of psychoanalysis was the fact that one participated in it lying down. Wherever I am I tend to gravitate toward the nearest couch or sofa, so this aspect of the treatment coincided with my natural predilections. My psychiatrist had a secretary-nurse who was completely nuts and I gathered that he was also analyzing her. The psychiatrist was himself in the 18th year of analysis with another analyst. He thought it was all great fun.

He was always smoking a cigar and he looked to me just like a successful businessman which, indeed, he was. In addition to being a medical practitioner, he was on the board of some advertising company as a psychological adviser.

Off his consulting room he had another room, in which stood a weird electrical gadget. It had chromium-plated bars to which one was induced to hold on. It gave one a mild electric shock which was supposed to calm the nerves; it just made me feel more nervous. This contraption looked just like one of those things you find at fun fairs and I would not have been unduly surprised to learn that that was where he had, in fact, found it.

You entered his office by one door and left by another—this was to avoid the embarrassment of encountering your friends coming in as you were going out.

He was a very friendly, chatty sort of psychiatrist and he would frequently spend a large amount of my fifty-dollar hour telling me funny stories about his other patients. If he wasn't really worth fifty dollars an hour as a psychiatrist, he certainly was as a funnyman, but after 3 months his material was becoming a bit stale and I left.

My second psychiatrist was a Jungian and he seemed almost exclusively concerned with my dreams. I had always been a rather modest dreamer, but by the time I got through with this man my dreams had become Cecil B. DeMille productions. It was the least I could do for him. To have given him my meager little dreams to analyze and interpret would have been a waste of his extraordinary talent and my money. So I tried very hard to dream things worthy of his genius; instead of merely dreaming about drowning in my bathtub I dreamed of great floods which encompassed the earth, of finding refuge on Noah's Ark, of confronting Moses on Mount Sinai and Moses parting the flood, purely for my benefit, as he had parted the Red Sea. The film rights of my dreams must have been worth a fortune.

But none of this explained why I had developed a backache at the thought of having to appear for 15 months in South Pacific.

It was clear to me that drastic action was required; my defenses were too strong for most of these boys to pierce and the prospect of spending 15 months on a couch was even less alluring to me than the prospect of 15 months on the stage.

My next choice of psychiatrist was a hypnotherapist. His objective was to put me to sleep. Now normally, I am most willing and anxious to go to sleep at any conceivable opportunity. I can sleep through thunderstorms, concerts, plays, films, after-dinner speeches, and even Zsa Zsa's parties with the greatest of ease. I can sleep standing up, sitting, lying down, and, I sometimes suspect, driving a car. But when my unfortunate hypnotherapist tried to put me to sleep, he failed miserably.

He began by explaining his system to me. All he wanted me to do was to pick out a spot, actual or imaginary, on the ceiling of his consulting room and keep staring at it without blinking. At the same time I was to relax completely and not fight him. He explained that one could not be hypnotized unless one co-operated and therefore I must not resist in any way. Also one had to be intelligent. Presently my eyeballs would begin to feel very prickly, my eyelids would become heavy, and I would fall into a light trance. He pointed out that I had nothing to fear about the hypnotic state since I could not be made to do anything against my natural inclinations or of which my moral sense disapproved. This did not reassure me particularly as my natural inclinations are limited only by the broadest horizons and my moral sense scarcely exists. However, I was anxious to co-operate and I said I would do my best. As I have said, I am always willing to go to sleep.

I sat on a chair in the middle of the room with the hypnotherapist behind me, out of sight. I found myself a spot on the ceiling and stared at it hard. Behind me, the hypnotherapist was talking softly in a monotonous voice. "That's it now, relax. Sit very relaxed. Relax your neck muscle, relax your chest muscle, relax your stomach muscle, relax your thigh muscle, relax your ankle muscle. Keep very relaxed. Relax your neck muscle, relax . . ." He kept on intoning the same phrases continuously.

How on earth, I thought, do you relax your ankle muscle? I hadn't even been aware that one had an ankle muscle. I tried to find it so that I could relax it. But by this time we were back to the neck muscle, and anxious to co-operate, I left the ankle unrelaxed and concentrated on the neck. But we were going too fast and I had no sooner located something that might conceivably have been a neck muscle before we were down to the ankle again—with all my chest

muscles, stomach muscles, thigh muscles, completely neglected. In my efforts to find the right muscles to relax, I
twisted and turned on the chair like a contortionist. Of
course, while all this was going on I had completely forgotten
about staring at the spot on the ceiling, and that ruined
everything. We had to start again.

This time I cheated. Ashamed to admit that I had no idea
of where all my various muscles were situated, and that I
was therefore incapable of relaxing them, I did nothing. I
merely stared at the spot on the ceiling. I was delighted to
find that after a while my eyes actually did begin to feel
prickly: at least I wasn't a complete duffer, I could manage
that part of it. The psychotherapist, obviously pleased with
my progress, was saying: "Your eyes are feeling very prickly
now, very prickly. They are very tired. Don't fight it. Relax
your neck muscle, relax your chest muscle," etc., etc.

My eyes were beginning to water and I tried hard not to
blink: things were getting a bit fuzzy.

"That's it," said the hypnotherapist, "your eyelids are very
heavy now, very heavy. You can scarcely keep them open.
Your eyelids are terribly heavy. You are feeling very tired."

The truth of the matter was that my eyelids didn't feel
the least bit heavy and I had never felt less tired in my life,
but I felt it would be rather impolite to tell him this since
it would amount to calling him a liar.

"Close your eyes," he said, "don't fight it, your eyelids
are very heavy, you can't keep them open. Close your eyes,
don't fight it."

I felt it would be churlish to refuse and so I closed my
eyes.

"Now," said the psychotherapist, "you are in a light
trance."

"As a matter of fact . . ." I murmured.

"Don't fight it," he said.

"Oh, all right," I said.

"In a little while," said the psychotherapist, "I am going to tell you to open your eyes and then you will be out of the trance. When you wake up, you will feel much better."

I lifted my eyelids slightly and took a peep at the room just to make sure I wasn't dreaming that I was awake when I was really asleep as the hypnotherapist claimed. But I had no difficulty opening my eyes, and according to him this should have been impossible until he had given me the word.

However, he seemed so pleased to have eventually put me to sleep that I thought it would be a pity to spoil things for him. I closed my eyes again and listened.

"When you wake up," he was saying, "you will feel much happier, your anxieties will have diminished, you will feel fresh and relaxed. All your problems will seem much smaller. You will have more confidence in yourself. You will be able to use your great natural talents to the full. Your performances on the screen will become even more brilliant than they are already . . ."

At this stage I was thinking that it would have been a pity to have been asleep and have missed such delightful eulogies. If this was his technique, I could understand why he was so popular with actors. He went on in the same vein for several minutes, his praise of my genius, my charm, my personality, becoming increasingly fulsome. If I had not remembered in time that I was supposed to be asleep I would have done the only decent thing and blushed. Eventually the praise and reassurance came to an end and he said, "Now I shall count three and when I say the word three you will open your eyes. You won't remember anything of what I have said, but you will feel pleasantly relaxed and generally much happier and healthier. One. Two. Three."

I opened my eyes and turned to him.

"Well," he said, "how d'you feel?"

"Fine," I said, "but I feel—I hope you won't take this amiss—but I feel I must tell you I wasn't really asleep."

"You just think you weren't," he said, beaming, "but I can assure you you were."

"Really," I said, "I ought to know whether I was asleep or not. As a matter of fact, I can remember everything you said —including the fact that your last remark was that I wouldn't remember anything."

"Ah well, that doesn't matter," he said. "It's been very beneficial."

"Oh indeed," I agreed, "and I must thank you for all the kind things you said about me. You are too generous."

"Oh, not at all," he said.

After the hypnotherapist, I decided I would have to try something more unconventional. I went to see a man who did not believe in Freud, Jung, Adler or hypnotism. He didn't even believe in aspirins. He was a very intelligent-looking man though he had for some inexplicable reason failed, or neglected to pass, any of the recognized medical examinations.

He listened very attentively to my whole story. Then he removed his glasses, momentarily buried his face in his hands and re-emerged to make his pronouncement: "You are," he said, "suffering from the sickness of our age."

"And what is that?" I inquired.

"Cynicism," he said.

"Why should that give me a backache?" I asked.

"Its consequences are far-reaching," he said.

"Well, what do I do about it?"

He looked at me with his big compassionate eyes and muttered one word—"Love."

"Anyone in particular?" I asked.

"Everyone," he said. "It's the only solution. You must love everyone—the girl at the cigarette stand, the elevator boy, the policeman on the corner, the head of the studio, your co-stars. Everyone. I know it's hard, but you must make the effort."

"But," I protested, "my whole career is based on being a character who is cynical and suave. I can't start playing Bing Crosby roles at my time of life."

"Career," he said, "that's not important. The world is destroying itself with materialism. It is prostrating itself before the golden calf of the dollar. You must return to the basic rhythms of life—to simplicity."

"Does that mean I have to give up my refrigerator, my car, my TV set?"

"You don't need them," he said.

"And my valet?" I asked.

"You don't need him," he said.

"You mean I have to press my own suits, cook my own breakfast, wash the car—oh, I'm sorry, I forgot, I've given up the car."

"None of these things are important," he said, "when you have learned to love."

"Well, that's very interesting," I said. "I'll think about it."

"It's the only way," he said. And I got up to leave.

"That'll be seventy-five dollars," he said.

"Why seventy-five?" I asked. "All the others only charge fifty dollars an hour."

"It's part of the treatment," he said. "It will help you attach less importance to money and material things."

One of the acknowledged difficulties about being cured of anything by a psychiatrist is that, since basically one does not want to be cured, one seeks out those practitioners of this delicate science who are least likely to cure you, of whom, I may say, there is an abundant supply. As a matter of fact most people in distress are more interested in being comforted than being cured.

I had already wasted several months on several couches and all I had learned was that I obviously did not want to be cured. I had been going to psychiatrists of my choice, and as my choice in these matters was patently suspect, I decided I had better go to somebody I didn't want to go to.

Zsa Zsa had been urging me for some time to see her own analyst and I had been strenuously resisting this suggestion —she was on such good terms with him, he liked her so much, that I feared he would merely be a source of continual propaganda for her, with me as a captive audience. I heard enough of Zsa Zsa's innumerable virtues from her and I had no desire to receive scientific corroboration of their existence. Nonetheless, feeling like a man walking into an ambush, I made an appointment to see her analyst.

Zsa Zsa's taste in psychiatrists, as in other spheres, turned out to be exemplary. He was one of the best. In due course he not only cured me of my obsessional impulses and my periodic backaches but he also cured me of Zsa Zsa.

The treatment began with sodium pentathol injections which have the effect of breaking down one's resistance and making one talk freely. For a period of several months I talked and he listened and interpreted, and eventually I began to gain some insight into the workings of my psyche. I learned that I was, to use the technical jargon, an obsessional compulsive, my marriage to Zsa Zsa having been a typical manifestation of this trait. You may not consider that an obsessional compulsion to marry Zsa Zsa is, per se, a sign of neurosis, and indeed, I feel sure there must be some men who, married to Zsa Zsa, were completely balanced. But my marriage to Zsa Zsa was just one of many impulsive actions which couldn't be explained on any logical basis. My sudden desire to get out of my contract with Rodgers and Hammerstein fitted into the over-all pattern of compulsive-obsessional behavior.

Then there was the odd business of my teeth. Like a great many Hollywood actors, I had allowed a dentist to put jackets on my teeth. This went against all my deepest convictions as I have always held one should not muck around with what Nature has given one, however miserly Nature may have been in the first place. I have always disapproved of aging actors having face-lifts or of girls having their noses shortened or their breasts enlarged. These things offend me aesthetically; one does not take the Mona Lisa to a commercial artist so that he can paint in a cute nose if that happens to be currently fashionable.

And yet, though it went completely against the grain for me, I had allowed a dentist to put jackets on my teeth. Once it was done I suffered agonies of remorse; it may seem a very trivial matter but it caused me to feel profoundly depressed.

When I began to look into my various actions in the light of the psychological knowledge I was acquiring, I discovered that many of the things I had done could only be explained in terms of a profound need on my part for self-punishment. On this basis the business of my teeth and my rejection of the Rodgers and Hammerstein offer suddenly made sense. And so did my marriage to Zsa Zsa. It also explained why I had made some of the films I did.

All my life I had been doing things that were clearly against my best interest; now I was beginning to find out why.

In our youth we are all inculcated with what I consider a totally superfluous sense of guilt; and so we continually expect punishment for our actions and only feel good when we have had our quota of punishment. Later when there is no father or mother around to punish us, we make up this deficiency by punishing ourselves. We just have to be punished by someone.

Having made these somewhat basic discoveries, I found life much easier. Nowadays, I am on much better terms with myself and am learning to view my few failings with infinite compassion.

Because I have at times treated psychiatry rather lightly, this does not mean I belong to that misguided majority who regard the whole subject with derision and contempt. That I needed to see five psychiatrists before finding one that suited me should not be considered a criticism of the profession. I happen to be very choosy, and I have had far more trouble finding a shirtmaker who suited me. There are, of course, charlatans and others who are merely incompetent and still others who are undoubtedly mad. But many of them are brilliant and dedicated men and their discoveries about the human mind are of supreme importance. Some of them are also perfectly sane. If human beings are ever to find any kind of peace they must learn how to live with one another and with themselves. This will only be possible when everyone has some knowledge of the motives, the compulsions and the impulses which determine his behavior. I think it is of far greater importance for schoolchildren to be taught psychology than mathematics. I would go further and say that all children should go through some form of analysis as part of the school curriculum. If they are healthy, well-adjusted children, it will be instructive and intellectually beneficial to them. If they are maladjusted, it will be possible to straighten them out at a time when this is still a comparatively simple matter.

Of course the adoption of such a progressive idea might have the effect of depriving future generations of such outstanding personalities as Mr. Hitler, Mr. Nietzsche, Mr. Kafka and Mr. Sanders. This loss, grievous though some might consider it, could I think be borne by the world without undue hardship.

CHAPTER 10

SHORTLY AFTER ZSA ZSA and I were mar-
ried, I received an offer to do a picture in Spain. It was to
be directed by the great French *metteur-en-scène,* Julien du
Vivier, and the cast was to include Herbert Marshall, Agnes
Moorhead, Marcelle Darieux, and José Nieto. The principal
actors were to be paid out of the receipts of the picture, but
they were to receive traveling and living expenses throughout the production.

The shooting schedule was to be eight weeks, and the location—the island of Mallorca.

It was the sort of project against which Hollywood actors
were being warned, as a number of such ventures had resulted in a great loss of time, a lot of grief and no profit.
But things were slack in Hollywood and the offer was opportune. It would in any case be a sort of honeymoon, and
who was to say—there was always a chance that the picture

might make some money and that I would get paid. It was in a frame of mind conditioned by these considerations that I accepted the deal.

In a somewhat lighthearted mood we flew to Paris and installed ourselves in a very elegant suite at the Hôtel Plaza Athenée. The producer, who called upon us later in the day, went a little green around the gills when he observed the sumptuous nature of our appointments, but since our contract called for him to defray first-class expenses, he was not in a position to offer any comment on the situation other than to express, with thinly veiled sarcasm, the hope that we would be comfortable.

From Paris we took the train to Barcelona, and thence we proceeded by air to Mallorca, where the whole company was billeted at the Hotel Mediterraneo.

I was filled with foreboding from the start.

The first assistant director was, according to my informants, none other than the real Mike Romanoff, His Imperial Highness Prince Michael of all the Russias, who was accompanied by Annabella. The second assistant was bemonocled Count Almos Mezo a former Hungarian diplomat, who affected the squeaky boots that were traditional in the hussar regiment to which he had once been attached. The gallantry of the Hungarian hussars called for an officer and a gentleman always to wear squeaky boots so as not to surprise his lady.

I began to get a feeling I was to recognize many years later with Rossellini, a feeling that the atmosphere surrounding the picture was somewhat deficient in what I might call the serious approach to movie-making. This feeling grew stronger in me as time went by and very little work was done. The story was about a man who had a yacht which he used to smuggle dope from Tangiers. The company rented a sixty-foot cabin cruiser from the coast guard, and it was our custom to put to sea every morning from the yacht club in Palma, and cruise around the island until we found a suitable spot to start shooting. But the director and the cameraman, bent upon making a masterpiece, would not shoot unless the sky was exactly to their liking, which to my way of thinking, happened rather seldom.

On one occasion I was standing on the quay at the yacht club waiting for our boat to be warped alongside when I noticed a trim white craft, flying an English yacht club pennant and obviously making for the dock where I was standing. I watched it maneuver gracefully into mooring position and since I had nothing else to do, I lent a hand in the business of securing the boat to the dock. A tall Englishman emerged from the wheelhouse and thanked me for my efforts on his behalf. We got into conversation and struck up a casual friendship. He turned out to be, in real life, the character that I was portraying in the picture; namely, a dope smuggler from Tangiers. After he got through telling me the problems of his adventurous life, his close shaves with the coast guard, the tension, the constant vigilance, the betrayals and the ever haunting fear of being caught, I came to the conclusion that it was much more comfortable to act him, than to be him.

I must confess that at first I found our strange method of picture-making very pleasant. It virtually amounted to straight yachting with practically no work. However, the days soon turned into weeks and the weeks into months. The eight-week schedule evaporated when we were only one-third of the way through the picture. The company was becoming extremely restive. The producers, practically without funds, were even worrying about how to pay our hotel bills. Zsa Zsa, who had been unable to stand the monotony of the hotel room and had pushed off to Paris for a couple of weeks, now returned to find the situation no better than when she left.

At about the same time, Count Almos Mezo, our distinguished second assistant director, also returned to take up his arduous duties once again. He had absented himself for a few days to relieve the monotony of his own life, which he had sought to accomplish by fox-hunting on his estates near Paris. He was met upon his arrival at the airport with full honors by His Imperial Highness, Prince Michael of all the Russias, and Annabella.

Toward the end of the fifth month my own morale reached an all-time low. I had become convinced that we would never get off the island, that I was doomed to stay there for the rest of my life. From the balcony of my hotel room I could see the Bellever Castle where Archduke Ferdinand of Austria was said to have died of a broken heart after living there in exile for a number of years. He must have been far more comfortably situated than I, since he was waited on hand and foot by his retainers and enjoyed the run of the island and the best of its food. His living conditions were infinitely superior to those which we had to put up with at the hotel, but this was obviously not enough—a man does not live by bread alone. An intolerable nostalgia finally brought about his demise. It must have been the sort of nostalgia that was beginning to grow in me.

It had become my custom to sit on my balcony every evening and look out across the harbor at the white-hulled steamer that sailed every night for Barcelona. I would watch the passengers embarking. They seemed to be so carefree and gay that I longed to be one of their number. Occasionally, the general wharfside din, the clamor of the porters and the warning blasts of the ship's whistle would rise above their excited chatter, but nothing would impede their triumphant progress.

Presently, the ship would leave and pass within a stone's throw of my balcony and I could see through its brightly lit portholes into the cozy cabins within. The music from the ship's orchestra, mingling with the laughter of the passengers, would drift across to me and increase my torment.

As the ship left the harbor it would give one final blast from its whistle, by which time I would be straining over the balcony. The whistle was a siren's song to my ears and I was Ulysses, lashed to the mast. I would feel wild, unreasoning emotions surging through me, and there was born in me an overwhelming determination to get on board that ship, come what may.

I telephoned my agent in California to find out if there were not some way in which I could break free from my contract. He informed me that my contract had already been technically breached by the producer as a result of his failure to pay certain sums of money that were owing to me. I seized upon this fact with fingers of steel. The hour of my liberation had come. I could now be sure that I was not going to suffer the same fate as the Archduke Ferdinand.

I took my contract to a Spanish lawyer who drew up a long, imposing document, covered with seals and stamps. I then went down to the shipping office and bought two tickets for Barcelona. I had no clear idea of what I was going to do after I reached my destination and nothing could have concerned me less. My only objective was to get on board that ship. I made my way back to the hotel and ran into the producer in the lounge. I stopped him and handed him my impressive-looking document and made a short explanatory speech concerning the nature of its contents. He received it with a bewildered and crestfallen expression, and while I felt for the safety of the boat tickets in my pocket, the look on his face made my heart bleed for him. I attempted to assuage his feelings by pointing out that if he did not finish the picture nobody would ever know how great a failure it was going to be, that while his backers would certainly lose the money they had already invested, at least they would be guaranteed against the much greater loss they would incur if they went ahead and finished the picture. He did not seem to be convinced by my argument, but I was impatient to be on my way and did not feel disposed to labor the point.

I found Zsa Zsa upstairs executing an oil painting of the harbor. I explained the situation to her and told her to start packing. She looked at me with an expression that clearly indicated she thought I had lost my mind—which indeed I had—but she did not try to dissuade me. She fell right in with my mood and started packing. Whatever else could be said about Zsa Zsa, and a great deal could, and is, being said about her, one thing is certain, she has a lot of guts. Our packing concluded, she telephoned the Herbert Marshalls and invited them to see us off on the boat. They accepted with alacrity, and without questioning our actions, fell in with our mood. They gallantly brought up the rear as we majestically strode through the atmosphere of despair that permeated the lounge, imperiously brushed our way past the strained white faces that were now crowding the vestibule, and triumphantly swept through the swing doors and out of our hotel prison into sweet fragrant freedom and the Mediterranean night.

By the time we reached the dock we were in a mood of irrepressible gaiety. We were the first passengers up the gangway and so had plenty of time to toast our guests in champagne. We toasted freedom and friendship; we toasted love. Then we started toasting absent friends, collectively and individually. Finally, the ship's whistle blew and we said good-by. As we steamed out of the harbor our eyes became riveted upon our hotel balcony—fascinated. It seemed quite unreal to be looking in the opposite direction from that to which we had by now and for so long become accustomed.

We had a smooth, pleasant, and uneventful crossing. Upon arrival in Barcelona the next morning we drove to the hotel where we found numerous messages awaiting us, imploring us to return. Later in the day we received a visit from none other than Count Almos Mezo, who had flown in, squeaky boots and all, from Palma as the company's plenipotentiary. He was white-faced and trembling, but his diplomatic training stood him in good stead—he said all the right things. We had a short, rather tight-lipped discussion, sitting on gilt chairs in the ballroom of the hotel, at the end of which I agreed to resume work.

We flew back to Palma that afternoon and were met with full honors by His Imperial Highness, Prince Michael of all the Russias—and Annabella. We found that a salutary change had been brought about by my defection. A new determination had been born to speed up the shooting of the picture and get it over with. From then on things seemed to go much faster, although two whole months were to elapse before the picture was finally completed. One of these was spent in Madrid and the other in Paris, and both were a decided improvement over the five preceding ones. Our morale was raised partly by the fact that Madrid and Paris were welcome changes from the provincial atmosphere of Mallorca, and partly because one could see the light at the end of the tunnel.

When it was finished and we were at last free to go back to our homes in America, nothing had been gained except freedom. A number of backers had been ruined and a lot of precious time had been lost. None of the artists were paid for their services and nothing was gained by anybody, other than the comforting knowledge that, at long last, it was over.

CHAPTER 11

ONE OF THE MOST USEFUL discoveries I've made in the fifty-three years I've been wandering about the surface of this planet has been the writings of Dr. Eric Fromm, who pointed out in one of his enlightening books that if life is to be successfully lived one must try to make an art of living.

Until I realized this fact to the full, many of the activities in which I found myself engaged were not really to my liking, and many of the people with whom I associated were not altogether of my choosing.

I seemed to be burdened with obligations to people whose welfare need not have been my concern. Dr. Fromm made the observation that people spend the greater part of their lives learning the various arts they need to master in order to insure their survival, without ever giving a thought to the most important art of all, the simple art of living.

Since everybody seemed to be in the same boat, I began to realize that if I could find the courage to swim against the current of popular opinion, I might be able to remedy the situation as far as I personally was concerned.

This thought led me to the conclusion that the very first step would be to learn how to say NO! How to say no to people and things I didn't want.

I began to reason that my habit of saying yes on nearly all occasions—a habit which, I need scarcely say, was always getting me into difficulties—stemmed from an early child-hood training that taught me to please grownups at all times. When I was very small, the grownups around me seemed to be omnipotent giants upon whose tolerant approval I depended for my very life. To please them seemed to be my only chance for survival. If I said yes to them they would smile and give me candy. If I said no they would punish me. It's strange how the fear of punishment lingers. With some people it remains until quite late in life.

Nowadays I find I am able to say NO to people who try to raise their own self-esteem by lowering mine.

I can say NO to people who give me advice only because they want to prove themselves wiser, and thereby exercise domination over me. I do not feel compelled to sacrifice myself and say yes merely to please another person. Therefore, before giving my answer in such a situation I say to myself, "I am not a child, therefore I don't need to go out of my way to please grownups in order to guarantee my survival. If I do not please myself, I please no one." If I make a habit of saying yes when the answer is no, I shall not only lose my own self-esteem but in the end I shall also lose the esteem of the person I'm trying to please. Before I broke myself of the habit of saying yes when I should have said no, the loss of self-esteem I'd incur would reveal itself to me in the form of a general feeling of unworthiness. I would begin to hate myself. I would look out of the window and the world would look gray. I would begin to hate the world.

But once I learned how to say no, all kinds of wonderful things began to happen. I felt at ease. I found greater capacity for making friends and less apprehension toward making enemies. In short, I was a doll.

Whenever I return to New York after a stay in Europe, I invariably get the feeling that America needs European aid. No matter how luxurious a suite I engage for myself, in no matter which first-class hotel, I feel that I am in an underprivileged country. There are no buttons that I can press to summon servants to do my bidding. There is only a telephone by which I can communicate with the reluctant members of the hotel staff—and I hesitate to use it because I am expecting calls from my friends.

I would like the valet to unpack my bags, but I can only reach him by telephone, and if I succeed in getting through to him, a gruff voice will ask me if I want my pants pressed. He will not understand that while I am perfectly capable of unpacking my bags myself, there are other uses to which I might prefer to put my time.

I am hungry. If I call room service, I know it will be busy and I cannot afford to sit with the phone off the hook, because, in addition to the calls from my friends, I am expecting an important call from California. Eventually, I give up and unpack my own bags. Eventually I telephone the valet to pick up some of my suits that need pressing. Eventually I telephone room service and finally get through to them. I receive some of my calls—the few that came through when my phone was not busy—and then go into the bathroom to take a shower.

Room service arrives with the meal I have ordered while

I am in the shower. Unlike the system employed in European hotels, the waiter is not allowed to open your door with a pass-key, roll in the table and go out, shutting the door quietly behind him. I have to get out of the shower, go to the door dripping wet, and let him in. Get back into the shower again, finished my ablutions, dry myself on a towel provided by the hotel that is only a little larger than a pocket handkerchief, go back into the sitting room where I find the waiter still hanging about, waiting for me to sign the check —an instrument of mutual mistrust which serves no useful purpose other than to guarantee the waiter's tip.

The American tip is in no sense a gratuity. It is regarded by its recipient as his due, his inalienable right. To the donor it is a safeguard against the latent ill-nature of the recipient. It is grudgingly given and condescendingly received. But so much for a deplorable pernicious tribal custom.

I now sit down to eat and reach for the coffeepot. The American hotel coffeepot has been designed with marvelous cunning. It is so constructed that no coffee emerges from it until a critical angle of tilt is achieved, at which point the lid flies open and the coffee spills all over the tablecloth and your trousers, singeing the skin beneath. This, of course, can be avoided by holding the knob of the lid with the left hand while pouring with the right. The knob, as to be expected, is so hot that you burn your fingers. Hotels in this respect are very fair and provide you with a straight choice —you either burn your fingers or you burn your knees, but in no cricumstances can you come out of the operation unscathed.

There was, of course, a time when coffeepots in American hotels were constructed in a manner consistent with the convenience of their users, but such a state of affairs could not be permitted to survive the diabolical machinations of industrial designers. Years of painstaking research must have been required to calculate the delicate balance between the viscosity of the coffee and the shape of the edge of the lid, so that it would seat down and trap the air within the pot for the required length of time.

I finish my meal in due course and communicate this outstanding piece of information to room service by telephone, so that they can remove the table. I then go into the bedroom and there, in a state of exhaustion occasioned by the stress of my domestic activities, cast myself on the bed.

The bed is six inches too short for me and my feet hang over the end. I am not average height. I am above average height, and therefore, no provision for my comfort is made. In America you must either be average in every way or have a hard time. By pulling the mattress down a foot from the headboard and stuffing pillows into the gap, I manage to get a fairly good night's sleep.

I am, of course, awakened a number of times during the night by offstage noises which last until about four o'clock in the morning, at which time the heating is mysteriously shut off and one freezes into wakefulness.

The offstage noises are the result of an artful collaboration between the architects of the hotel, who manage to locate one's next-door neighbor's bathroom no more than a six-inch wall's width from the headboard of one's bed, and the desk clerks, who see to it that one's neighbor is a person who has contracted amoebic dysentery.

CHAPTER 12

I OFTEN WONDER IF I really need a telephone. Is it a convenience or is it a nuisance? Perhaps it is as much one as it is the other. I am ambivalent about it. About my television set, I am less ambivalent. I know I don't need it. I have been a slave to its novelty for the past seven years, but now that this novelty has worn off I find that I only turn it on occasionally when something very special is being presented. (Such as myself.)

About my car I am pathologically ambivalent. I know that I must work hard to support it, but from the residential district where I happen to live I cannot conveniently get to work without it.

My washing machine, my deep freeze, my electric dishwasher, my Waring mixer, my refrigerator and my electric garbage disposal unit belong to a more recondite part of my life. Consequently it is more difficult for me to appraise the value of the contribution that these devices make toward my comfort. I am aware only that they cost money and require constant maintenance.

Modern conveniences are the source of modern inconveniences. They create as many problems as they solve.

I am sometimes tempted to load my Hi-Fi, my radio alarm clock, and all the other parasitical devices of which I am the irresolute possessor, into my car and drive them— and my car—over a cliff and be done with it.

If there were some foreseeable end to technological improvement, if we could only say "Let's call a halt at such and such a point of technical excellence, and from there on we will go no farther," I would be a wholehearted subscriber to the system whose goal was to reach that point at the earliest possible moment.

But the system we have chosen can lead only to further enslavement to an ever mounting assortment of devices, the workings of which we do not understand and must depend upon others to keep in good repair.

When I travel abroad and find myself in the company of people who belong to a society that is denied the so-called benefits of modern technology, I get along very well. I find that I rediscover to some extent the lost art of conversation and enjoy once again such simple primordial pleasures as going for a walk, sitting by the fire or reading a book. Consequently I wonder if there is any point in being up-to-date.

America is the yardstick by which progress throughout the world is measured. I sometimes think back to the America I knew twenty years ago and wonder if its people are any happier today than they were then, and if its products, though infinitely more variable in number and ingenious in design, are as durable, as honestly made and as desirable in terms of things one wants to possess.

America, more than any other country, is a culture of

group pressures. The desire to conform is very strong and the approval of the herd is assiduously sought. Advertising men exploit these facts relentlessly. The welfare and happiness of the group is never for a moment considered. Their sole aim is to bring about an ever increasing consumption of totally unnecessary products.

The obsolescence principle, the motivational research principle and the subliminal perception principle would appear to have been invented only to improve methods whereby people are cynically induced to shackle themselves to pay for things they do not need out of money they do not have.

Ever since the dawn of mass production, the quality of manufactured products has deteriorated in direct proportion to their diffusion throughout the community. Cars are getting tinnier every year. If you turn any of the knobs on your dashboard a little too heartily it is more than likely to come off in your hand. I am always surprised that the door does not fall off when you open it, although I am sure that this will be arranged for us someday by Detroit.

The art of the individual craftsman is now no longer known in America. If one wants something rather special one has to have it made in one of the "Backward Countries."

I am ineluctably drawn to the gloomy conclusion that the genius of the American people will drive them into ever tightening bonds of enslavement to technological progress. Out of this the machine will emerge triumphant, man will concern himself exclusively with its maintenance, and we shall all sing, "Oh say, does that star-spangled banner still wave O'er the land of TV and the home of the slave."

CHAPTER 13

SOME TIME AGO I was staying with one of my upper-class friends who lives in a castle.

Being very much in favor of having friends so well situated in life, I gave him my full attention when he confided his woes to me.

"For instance," he complained, "I have to have a permanent mason to keep the place up." He meant of course literally "up."

While I digested this seemingly grand remark, my mind began to wander in the direction of my own difficulties in this regard.

Consider the people I have to employ to keep me "up," I thought. The people that cut my hair, shave my face, clip my nails, fix my teeth, test my eyes, make glasses so that I can see, make clothes for me, prepare my food or represent me in legal, tax and business matters.

A sense of appalling injustice began to rankle in me. How is it possible in my life of austerity, simplicity, even ascetism, that I am incapable of functioning without this scaffolding to keep me "up"? And who, if it comes to that, is supporting whom? How did I in the prime of my life, healthy, hearty, able and tolerably willing, get into the same fix as a thirteenth-century castle?

Something sinister has happened in the conduct of modern life whereby one's time is divided between the excruciating bore of personal maintenance and the chronic necessity of signing papers relating to the general maintenance of one's position in society. My whole being became suffused with self-pity. "What a bloody outrage," I shouted.

My host turned to me with an expression of pleased surprise. "My dear fellow," he said, "I think it is very good of you to take my troubles so much to heart—let me give you another whiskey!"

"Ah, whiskey!" I reflected, gratefully moving my glass forward. "Whiskey is one of the few really enjoyable adjuncts to personal maintenance."

As I sipped it a large dog that had been sleeping in front of the fire languidly rose, yawned, stretched itself and started off toward the servants' hall with nothing in mind but oral pleasure and more sleep. I had the dismal prospect of climbing upstairs to my bedroom, getting undressed, hanging up my clothes, dressing in pajamas, brushing my teeth and cutting my toenails while the ladies of the house party would no doubt be engaged in the removal of superfluous hair, putting the hair that is not considered superfluous in curling pins, rubbing porridge into their hands and then putting on gloves, removing falsies and girdles and anointing various parts of their anatomy with strange chemicals, to mention only a few of the activities women have to engage in in order to keep their own personal "masonry" up.

It seems to me that we made a better job of it as arboreal apes and before that as nice neat fish.

I have invariably come away from visits to the zoo convinced that man is the ugliest of all living creatures with the possible exception of the hyena and the wart hog.

Yet even these misshapen beasts have over man an advantage which turns all of his cherished freedoms and vaunted intelligence into meager palliatives for his ineluctable dependency upon the burden of personal maintenance. In short, I would rather be a mule!

BOOK II

CHAPTER 1

ㅤ

E VERY AGE HAS ITS MADAME POMPADOUR, its Lady Hamilton, its Queen of Sheba, its Cleopatra, and I wouldn't be surprised if history singles out Zsa Zsa as the twentieth-century prototype of this exclusive coterie.

I never really met Zsa Zsa. We collided in New York at a party given by Serge Simonenko, the banker.

It was followed by a drink at her plush red satin draped penthouse apartment which set off a chain reaction of collisions. We collided in Bermuda, in Nassau, in Cuba, in Hollywood, and finally in Las Vegas where we also collided with a minister who put an end to all this nonsense with a ring.

Zsa Zsa was like champagne, and I as her husband was hard put to it to keep up with her standard of effervescence. I found her as difficult to communicate with as she was easy to collide with.

We were able to make contact on some levels; for example, we both had the same approach to humor, and we understood one another in certain aspects of our analysis of social life. But on certain rather important levels—how to live, for example—we were unable to communicate on the same wave length. We never arrived at a common set of values.

Of course it must be said in Zsa Zsa's defense that all women are difficult to communicate with since they can only think clearly while washing their hair.

After our divorce, Zsa Zsa and I enjoyed a much more harmonious relationship. We got along as friends infinitely better than we did as marriage partners. No one is a better date than Zsa Zsa. No one is a better companion on a trip even if it involves roughing it.

We traveled all over the United States and Europe together, sometimes in considerable discomfort, and I couldn't have wished for a more lighthearted, amusing and co-operative companion.

Zsa Zsa is perhaps the most misunderstood woman of our times. She is misunderstood because she is guileless. She allows her vitality and instincts to spring from her without distortion. She doesn't disguise her love of amorous entanglements or jewels or whatever else catches her fancy, because her character is pure. She is whole-cloth. An isotope of femininity. In a sense also radioactive and fissionable. Not for her is the conventional mask of studied behavior. Her behavior is spontaneous and genuine. The mask is used by people who want either to remain inviolate from the assaults of public life, or who need an invented glamour to conceal a more bovine interior. Zsa Zsa is too subjective for the former, and God knows she doesn't need the latter. I think that this kind of woman is intrinsically quite wonderful and doesn't deserve the somewhat contemptuous treatment to which she is all too frequently exposed simply because she doesn't fit into the accepted domestic pattern, which actually hardly fits anyone even if it is tolerated by most.

I don't see why domesticity should be the yardstick by which love, benevolence, good will and delight between men and women is judged. Neither do I see why all women who do not fit into the accepted pattern of domesticity should be branded as *femmes fatales*.

Actually, the real *femme fatale* is the modest, virtuous, self-sacrificing housewife—the so-called "good" woman. Her upbringing and training, buttressed by a thousand years of sly empiricism, is single-mindedly devoted to binding you ever tighter in the web of your guilt, which she mercilessly and unremittingly exploits.

If you come home late for dinner to such a woman she will not chide or admonish you, nor will she make a scene. With downcast eyes and Mona Lisa Smila she will kiss you gently on the forehead and make you feel like a murderer.

She will never make demands upon you but she will have a way of putting down her sewing and looking wistfully out of the window which will make you feel you ought to be making more money. Eventually she will divorce you, leaving your bank full of nothing but "guilt"-edged insecurities.

Life with such a woman is a perpetual apology which starts from the moment you meet her. By delicately declining your proffered cigarette she succeeds in making you feel guilty about smoking. You apologize and explain that you mean to give it up. Without pausing to savor her easily gained advantage, she artfully follows it up by moving the ashtray nearer to you. Nothing that a woman can do for a man will make him feel more secure than moving the ashtray nearer to him. I suppose it is subliminally symbolic of his nanny moving the pot toward him to sit on.

When a "good" woman drops her glove, looks into her bag, goes into the powder room, talks about your mother, or gamely tries to carry something that is obviously too heavy for her, it is part of her plan. Part of her strategy, part of her ineluctable spell. In short she is not to be trusted for a moment.

A woman who is really worth having is not necessarily good, clever, or virtuous herself. A really good woman will bring about a condition of good in you. "Good" being, of course, a state of happiness and contentment in which you can flourish and bloom and generally live to your fullest capacity.

One shouldn't delude one's self into thinking that the domestic paragon and splendid cook will fill this requirement. Common household services are better paid for in money than in marriage, which is liable to produce the disagreeable results of a grossly distended waistline coupled with conversation confined to comparative prices of ground beef.

Another perilous hazard which should be viewed with prudent reserve is the "iron maiden" of small services: having your letters typed, your bags packed, your shirts pressed, your plans made. This is the superfluous crutch which induces the affliction and relieves you of nothing so much as your independence.

If in spite of these warnings a man falls in love, he will encounter an additional set of problems.

To begin with, it is impossible to be in love with a woman without experiencing on occasions an irresistible desire to strangle her. This can lead to a good deal of ill-feeling. Women are touchy about being strangled. Then there is another point. While love may turn a man into a poet, it is more likely to turn him into a bankrupt, or what is worse a bore, and the primordial, jungle-type emotions it unleashes are hard to deal with in modern air-conditioned apartments.

The fact is that women should be worn like a boutonniere,

to add to one's look of distinction and contribute to one's air of charm and mood of gaiety. Delightful to pick and easy to replace, put on with pleasure, removed without pain, and remembered with the appreciative nostalgia normally reserved for those nice garlands they put round your neck in the South Seas, whose name for the moment escapes me.

I air these views gratuitously as I do not myself greatly care for boutonnieres or for that matter, women. If I were asked to express an opinion on the most aggravating feminine attributes—and God knows there would be a broad horizon of choice on such a subject—I would say that the two which have caused me the greatest exasperation and anguish are, one, that they are irresistible, and two, that they are irreplaceable.

CHAPTER 2

I T WAS A REMARK I MADE in *The Moon and Sixpence* which resulted in my acquiring a reputation as an authority on women. In the film I said—and they were Somerset Maugham's words, not mine—something to the effect that the more you beat women the better they were for it. I thought nothing of it at the time, but several months later, when I was making another film, I suddenly found myself in the center of a storm.

The Moon and Sixpence had been released and a whole mass of women were up in arms against me. They were outraged. "How could you have said such a thing?" they demanded with heaving breasts. "It was caddish, brutal, and uncivilized." In my defense I pleaded that I was only playing a part; the part of Gauguin who, after all, was caddish, brutal, and uncivilized. I begged them to see that I wasn't responsible for my own dialogue—I just spoke the words that were given to me. The fact that on this point Gauguin, Maugham and I were in unanimous accord was, in my opinion, neither here nor there.

In the course of several newspaper interviews, I facetiously embroidered on this theme. I said I approved of the oriental idea of keeping women in harems. I also said that you could treat women like dogs and they would still love you. Personally I always treat dogs with infinite courtesy, and indeed most men treat them better than they do their wives, but for some reason this was considered a disgraceful remark. All that was nearly 15 years ago, but the effect was far-reaching. Today, wherever I go, journalists still ask me if I am a woman hater. I have learned what sort of answers they expect and I do my best to provide them.

REPORTER: Mr. Sanders, what do you think of intellectual women?
ME: Are there any?
REPORTER: Do you think beautiful women make good wives?
ME: They make better mistresses. All women make better mistresses.
REPORTER: Do you think a woman should be beautiful before breakfast.
ME: It would never occur to me to look at a woman before breakfast.

Inevitably, in the 15 years or so that I have been making pronouncements on the subject of women, I have learned something about them. I found out as Jack Lemmon did in a recent movie, that they are a whole new sex.

Women of great beauty are the most baffling of the species, however, and since they abound in Hollywood a word about them would not be out of place.

"Beauty is only skin deep," as some dull clot once remarked. A very proper depth in my opinion. After all, who needs a beautiful gall bladder?

Hollywood sirens are constantly being accused of having beautiful faces and nothing behind them. The question is Why would we or they be better off if their faces were *plain* and had nothing behind them?

When I first met Hedy Lamarr, about twenty years ago, she was so beautiful that everybody would stop talking when she came into a room. Wherever she went she was the cynosure of all eyes. I don't think anyone concerned himself very much about whether or not there was anything behind her beauty, he was too busy gaping at her. Of her conversation I can remember nothing: when she spoke one did not listen, one just watched her mouth moving and marveled at the exquisite shapes made by her lips. She was, in consequence, rather frequently misunderstood. There may have been some who would have preferred her to be as plain as a school mistress and crisply articulate, but not I.

To many a beautiful woman her beauty is a religion, a vocation, a profession, and her life's work. To her, men are merely accessories which, if carefully chosen, enhance her beauty.

They act as a sort of mirror—which is why they are indispensable to her. In their faces she sees herself. Their desire is a reflection of her desirability. Their interest in her conversation is a reflection of her wit. Their love is a reflection of her endearing nature. As she sweeps through life, she will glance at men so that she may see mirrored in their faces all the virtues she believes she possesses.

Her life is a perpetual routine of beauty care; she is always being massaged, cosseted, pampered. She dares not drink or eat or stay up late. She is like some fabulous and fragile work of art that no one dares to touch. To some of her kind even making love is an activity she can only contemplate when it does not conflict with the requirements of her beauticians. But at least she can indulge in it at will. If she were plain, she might be left entirely to its contemplation.

Beauty is often spoken of by preachers and pessimists as in some way contemptible because it is ephemeral. There seems to be a gloomy satisfaction in the thought of its inevitable destruction. Is it then better to be permanently plain? Is it, come to think of it, possible to be permanently anything? A beautiful woman gets old. A plain woman gets plainer and old besides. This is not to say, however, that beauties hold all the cards in the pack. I have known quite a few plain women with remarkable capabilities.

But however much the beauties may suffer from the transitory qualities inherent in all aspects of life, I feel it my prerogative and pleasure to enjoy them as they come—and I go—even if my enjoyment falls short of the worship they prefer.

So anyway, there they are. Beautiful women—on whom so many words and hours and fortunes are spent, who are painted and pursued, adored and abused, married, and abandoned. Each one using this trump card in a different way. Like a joker in canasta, it is a powerful advantage properly played and a heavy load to have left in your hand.

Hedy Lamarr found it a load, whereas Marlene Dietrich took every trick in a tour de force of beauty. Greta Garbo's incandescent looks singed a generation of male moths but has apparently lasted to light only her own way. Dolores del Rio never found a better shrine at which to worship than her own. Elizabeth Taylor shares her ravishing beauty like a true patron of the poor with those who have none. Ava Gardner has ravaged a continent. Arlene Dahl opened a lingerie store. Clare Luce put pulchritude into politics and the Duchess of Windsor, to prove that beauty was at best a superfluous weapon, took the King of England unarmed. The variety is endless.

Then there are the ones who are not really beautiful at all, examined carefully—perhaps barely good-looking; but it is as if some attentive fairy godmother, observing the models to be of rather haphazard construction, had at the last minute thrown a bucket of beauty over them and sent them forth simply dripping with the stuff. Gertrude Lawrence was one of those who achieved a shimmering loveliness with a very indifferent face. Mrs. Bill Paley drifts about with her *fin-de-siècle* elegance, soaked with a beauty which really has no connection with her features. No one could say that Sylvia Ashley Fairbanks Stanley Gable Djordjadze's nose was a triumph of design, but her face and aura have produced enough brilliance to make a thousand chandeliers a fourth-rate illumination. It is all very confusing and all too successful in diverting the attentions of serious-minded men from their serious-minded objectives. However, to paraphrase Alice Duer Miller:

> In a world where beauty is finished and dead,
> I would not wish to live.

CHAPTER 3

DURING THE FIVE YEARS I was married to Zsa Zsa Gabor, I lived in her sumptuous Bel-Air mansion as a sort of paying guest. My presence in the house was regarded by Zsa Zsa's press photographers, dressmakers, the household staff, and sundry visitors and friends with tolerant amusement.

I was allotted a small room in which I was permitted to keep my personal effects until such time as more space was needed to store her ever-mounting stacks of press clippings and photographs.

I was accustomed to austerity and it was no great sacrifice for me to dispose from time to time of some of my belongings so as to empty drawers in my room and make them available for the more vital function of housing Zsa Zsa's memorabilia.

All of the tables, walls, cupboards and closets of various kinds were pressed into similar service.

Unless the hours on a picture I might be making were excessively long I would be home in time to stand at the bar under the large portrait of Zsa Zsa and fix drinks for her newspaper interviewers and photographers, who would be winding up a hard day. They would be most appreciative and would nod to me quite affably as I tended to their needs.

But the most rewarding experience would come later: driving the dressmaker home. She would always be extremely grateful.

Then there were the gay dinner parties, and occasionally the large catered parties with champagne, balloons, and tents, and a lot of rich gentlemen from South America.

It was a kaleidoscopic life and there were large areas of fun in it, yet there came a time when I felt I simply had to get away. Providence came to my assistance in the form of an offer from the great Italian director Roberto Rossellini to do a picture in Italy, co-starring with Ingrid Bergman.

Because of my tremendous respect and admiration for the well-known director, I accepted the offer with alacrity. I had recently seen some of his truly magnificent works, such as *Open City* and *Paisa,* and was eager to work with the man who could achieve such results. In addition, I was naturally looking forward to working with Bergman.

I sought out Zsa Zsa to inform her of my decision. I found her under the hair dryer going over the guest list for her next party. I managed to attract her attention by waving my passport in front of her and conveyed my intention of leaving for Italy in sign language—the noise of the hair dryer precluding conversation. She regarded me indulgently for a long moment and then with a sunny social smile returned to the sober scrutiny of her guest list.

To pack my bags was the work of a moment because my belongings by this time had shrunk to the barest essentials.

In no time at all I was in an airliner on my way to Rome.

I began to think again about the picture. My agent had told me there was no script, but this had caused me no particular concern because even in Hollywood I had often started on films without a script. Moreover the offer of the film had been so opportune as to outweigh any other considerations.

When I arrived in Rome, however, I was informed that there never would be a script. That is, it was not the Maestro's practice to shoot with a script. While I was somewhat bewildered by this knowledge, I felt that I had gone too far now to turn back, and that anyway perhaps insistence on a script for every picture was one of the things that was wrong with Hollywood. Certainly one way to insure that a script would not be bad would be to have no script at all.

It was in this somewhat pathologically jocular mood that I decided to persevere in the strange adventure, although my misgivings increased with every passing day.

For years I had been trained in the Hollywood tradition of efficient organization, of wardrobe plots, shooting schedules, and each man in a film crew having a specific task to perform. It came as no small surprise therefore to find that the Rossellini organization consisted simply of the great director himself and a number of assistants whose functions varied day by day. Some of them were sent on errands one day, and the next, given important work to do. A man of impressive appearance would one day be seen with brief case and important-looking papers and documents, and the following day in dungarees repairing the Maestro's skin-diving equipment.

When the day came to start shooting in Naples, I was in a state of such bewilderment that I asked Rossellini to release me from the picture, but to this he could not accede because money to back the film had been advanced on the basis of my being in it.

The first fortnight of shooting took place in the Naples

museum. Although I was not personally involved in any of these scenes—and it is even doubtful whether anyone else was in the final analysis—I went to the museum a number of times to watch the shooting. I am glad I did, for otherwise I probably would never have seen what are perhaps the most beautiful sculptures in the world.

The scenes filmed in the museum were a series of shots of Miss Bergman admiring the statuary. An octogenarian guide accompanied her giving a short dissertation on the merits of each statue they came to, while Miss Bergman nodded in mute appreciation.

While it did not seem to me that these scenes were making the most of Miss Bergman's very considerable talents as an actress, they were quite interesting to watch for the first few hours or so. By the end of two weeks, however, my interest was reduced to a state bordering on stupefaction.

Nevertheless, it was impossible to say what contribution these scenes made to the picture as a whole, as the story of the film was never understood at any time, by anyone, least of all the audience when the picture was released.

When it came my turn to appear in front of the cameras, the location was changed to a rented villa some twenty-five miles from Naples. It was late February and bitterly cold. There was no heating in the villa and there were no facilities or conveniences.

As there was no wardrobe plot to guide us, it often happened that I would arrive at the villa wearing the wrong clothes for the scene they were going to shoot. On such occasions they would drive me all the way to Naples to change my suit, then bring me back again, through the traffic, a total distance of about fifty miles and a total delay of at least two and a half hours. During the time I was gone, Rossellini and the crew would play cards and have a bottle of wine. Since we would usually start shooting at three o'clock in the afternoon and knock off at seven, not a great deal of work was accomplished during the day.

On one occasion I was told that a car would pick me up at two o'clock in the afternoon. This would have been fifteen minutes earlier than usual and my spirits rose accordingly. "Ah," I said to myself happily, "things seem to be picking up." Anxious to co-operate to the full in this faint but encouraging step toward efficiency, I stationed myself in the lobby of the hotel, eyes glued on the swing doors, ready, willing, and able.

When the clock struck three and the car had not appeared, I was disappointed but still undaunted. "Well," I said to myself, "they are going to be late, but at least a praiseworthy attempt has been made."

I sat and stared at the door. The afternoon wore on, the soft Neapolitan dusk flung a blue veil upon the snows of Vesuvius. Melodious cries of returning fishermen proclaimed the end of the day. The long white wings of circling gulls swept the sky like slender brushes painting it from a light to a darker blue.

I sat and stared at the door. Dinner guests came and went. I sat and stared at the door.

When the car finally came at four thirty A.M. the following morning I was unready, unwilling, unable, unshaven, and having lost all sense of proportion calling long distance to Zsa Zsa, who could not come to the phone anyway because she was under the hair dryer.

I was led like a man in Sing Sing's Death House to the waiting car which whisked me away to some Neapolitan back street where Rossellini had set up the camera to shoot the momentous scene for which we had all been waiting so patiently. He had his scarlet racing Ferrari with him and he kept eying it and stroking it while the cameraman was fiddling with the lights, getting the scene ready.

Finally when all was ready Rossellini changed his mind about shooting the scene and dismissed the thunderstruck company.

While we watched him in stupefied silence he put on his crash helmet, climbed into the Ferrari, gunned his motor, and disappeared with a roar and screeching tires round the bend of the street and out of our lives for two whole days.

It was his custom every once in a while to race the Naples–Rome Express, which I am told he invariably succeeded in beating.

This occasion was no exception, and when he returned two days later his triumph was only slightly dampened by a migraine headache he had acquired as a result of having had no sleep for forty-eight hours.

He retired to bed while the company sat around for another whole day waiting for him to recover.

We always had plenty of time for reflection and meditation on the picture and it was about this time that I began to wonder how the Maestro's strange ways were affecting Ingrid, and in just what stage *was* the romance that had rocked the world.

It would be hard to guess whether there was any real happiness in the relationship that existed at the time between Ingrid and Roberto, or whether in point of fact there ever had been.

It is common knowledge that their meeting was brought about indirectly as a result of the failure of the motion picture *Joan of Arc*. It was a very big flop and Ingrid suffered an emotional setback that produced in her a feeling of such insecurity that she needed someone to take over and run her life. It is said that she set forth her problem in letters to her favorite directors and that Rossellini, who was one of them, accepted the challenge.

Roberto was luxuriating at the time in the tremendous

success he had had with his two great pictures *Open City* and *Paisa* and could not have been aware of the dismal fact that he would never again be able to repeat his successes. A fact of which numerous Milanese financiers, to their subsequent chagrin and sorrow, were equally unaware.

Probably no European director shot up to such dizzy heights of fame so quickly as did Roberto Rossellini. He was received everywhere with the sort of reverence that is usually reserved for the Pope, or the Bell Telephone Company. Now to top this success he caught a lioness by the tail. A lioness in the shape of the number one movie actress of the day. It was enough to unhinge anybody.

The story of the romance that followed and the beautiful children it produced is as well known as the outraged reactions of the moralists. What is perhaps less well known is the psychological impact of each upon the personality of the other.

It was the talk of Italy that Roberto was ruining Ingrid by putting her into one bad picture after another; that he would not allow her to work for any other director, or see any movies except those made by him; and that he was, in short, devouring her in a sort of frenzy of possessiveness.

Yet although she was in tears a good many times during the making of the picture, it seemed to me that the very opposite was taking place. Far from being devoured, Ingrid was eventually to emerge triumphant, and Roberto was destined to bite the dust of obscurity, having improvidently exhausted his marvelous talent for raising money.

The opinion universally held among the well-informed was that Rosselini's insistence on shooting without a script was not only his madness but also his method of obtaining adequate financing for his tragic ventures.

Milanese industrialists, awed by his fame and swayed by

his charm, pressed money into Rossellini's hands as though it was something they didn't want.

Since there was no script, they assumed they were going to get another *Open City* or *Paisa,* both of which were shot in this way. Halfway through any picture he was shooting, Rossellini could always go to his backers and say that he had spent all the money and needed the same amount again to finish the picture.

His backers would not be in a position to replace him with another director because nobody else would be able to guess what the story was about.

I call his ventures tragic because they could so easily have been highly remunerative if he had operated in a normal manner.

He was not a man who really enjoyed working, and he hated to get up in the morning, a fact which he never tired of bringing to our attention. I wonder whether it is not sometimes as tantalizing to him as it always is to me to think how much more money he could have made by simply staying bed.

There was an occasion during the shooting of the picture when his predilection for not getting up in the morning was in perfect harmony with my own.

He had taken the entire company over to Capri to do some interior night shots that could have been done much more economically and easily in the studios in Rome. But of course one had to take into account the fact that the facilities for skin-diving in Rome were certainly not as good as those to be found in Capri.

After photographing the night scenes, Roberto decided he needed a shot of me arriving at the island by the steamer which used to dock around ten o'clock in the morning. Since he could not very well ask me to get up and go down to the dock when he was not prepared to do this himself, he instructed the cameraman to photograph any tall man getting off the boat.

On this particular morning the boat was crammed to capacity and about a thousand raucous jostling tourists disembarked while one of them, paid to wear my hat and coat, was successfully followed by the camerman.

Later Roberto decided he needed some shots of me on the boat to tie in with the one of my getting off it. For this he hired the entire steamer for the day. It was one of the most pleasant days from my point of view that I was to spend on the picture. The weather was glorious, I had the whole ship to myself, and was waited on hand and foot by the full complement of stewards who brought me *café con panna,* liqueurs, and sundry Italian delicacies. To save money, Rossellini had not hired any extras so that when the two sequences were cut together you first of all saw this singularly lonely man on a deserted ship making the crossing to Capri, then the ship arrives and a thousand passengers pushing and shoving each other succeeded in disembarking without ruffling the calm of the lonely tall man who now had unaccountably acquired a new face.

Rossellini was a great skin-diving *aficionado,* a fact which was mercilessly exploited by the crew on the picture. Whenever they felt they had done enough work for the day, one of the men would come running up to the great Maestro and, looking back over his shoulder with breathless excitement, point out to sea. "There!!! *Out there, out there!!!!"* he would cry. "A huge fish as big as this." And with arms outstretched and awestruck face he would stare at the spot on the water he had indicated earlier.

The effect on Rossellini of this little charade could not

have been more electrifying than if he had received a full-scale jolt of insulin shock treatment.

"Wrap it up," he would shout through teeth chattering with excitement, while with trembling hands he changed into his skin-diving outfit.

A few minutes later, with a loud plop and wiggling flippers, Rossellini's portly figure would disappear from view into the limpid waters of the Mediterranean, which would obligingly swallow him up for the rest of the day and relieve us of the burden of our chores.

But for all his eccentricities Rossellini was a very charming man, and he treated me with every consideration. When the picture finally came to an end I found myself strangely reluctant to part company with the flamboyant Roberto, the bravely smiling though tear-stained Ingrid, and the oddly assorted crew, and to take away with me to the south of France, where my plane was headed, only my memories of experiences that went to make up an adventure as full of odd surprises as it was replete with bewildering aggravations.

I arrived in Cannes and collided with Zsa Zsa, who had flown down from Paris where she had been the house guest of Diplomat Extraordinary His Excellency Don Porfirio Rubirosa, Dominican Ambassador to the Republic of France. She had met this colorful character in Deauville where he had apparently been resting up from the arduous tasks attendant upon the representation of his country's affairs by playing polo and exercising his fatal charm on the lady he was soon to marry, Miss Barbara Hutton.

After two weeks in Cannes where we went to all the parties, had lunch with the aging Aga Khan, gambled in the casinos, and generally had a very good time, I took off for Hollywood, and Zsa Zsa returned to Paris to assist in the promotion of good will between the Dominican Republic and France.

While I have always been a staunch supporter of International Accord, I found it a little hard to believe that the situation governing the relations between France and the Dominican Republic had become so crucial as to require the wholehearted co-operation of Hungarians.

Yet I know that I speak as a child in such matters and therefore I am inclined to leave them in the hands of the well-informed.

However, I did mention this matter rather briefly on my way through New York to Zsa Zsa's mother, the redoubtable Madame Jolie Gabor. Putting aside a pearl necklace she had been examining minutely through a magnifying glass, Madame Gabor looked at me in shocked surprise. "It is only *pour passer le temps*," she said, as though this explained everything. I left, more bewildered than ever, and caught a plane for Hollywood.

Albert, my butler, met me at the airport and drove me to Zsa Zsa's house where he unpacked my bags while I had a swim in the pool.

The house seemed to be much more spacious and serene than I had remembered it, and it was not long before I discovered the reason why—there were no photographers and dressmakers, no interviewers and no visitors.

I spent a couple of weeks in tranquil relaxation and then took Albert and my belongings on a search for an establishment of my own. I stopped at the first rentable house I came to in Pacific Palisades, moved in right away and lived in it temporarily for five years.

It was not long after I settled down in my new home that Zsa Zsa and I entered into divorce proceedings.

As I applied myself with ever-growing skill to the subtle art of living successfully as a bachelor I was reminded from time to time of the words of A. E. Housman:

Oh, when I was in love with you,
Then I was clean and brave,
And miles around the wonder grew
How well did I behave.

And now the fancy passes by,
And nothing will remain,
And miles around they'll say that I
Am quite myself again.

CHAPTER **4**

THE MOST INDISPENSABLE ADJUNCT to a happy life as a bachelor is money. For the poor it is on the whole better to be married, for a man must either have a wife or a servant to look after him, and the initial cost of a wife is usually within the means of a workingman, whereas to underwrite the direct and indirect costs of a good man servant in America one's financial resources must be roughly equal to those of the Prudential Life Insurance Company.

My butler, Albert, was as highly skilled in squeezing money out of his indulgent employer as he was in squeezing orange juice. He was as expert in the kitchen as he was adroit in the invention of excuses for being late on the mornings following his days off.

The best of these, and the one I cherish among my fondest memories, was that he had spent his day off in Tijuana where he had driven, in the car I provided for his use, to engage in a little harmless gambling at the casino, and due obviously to a case of mistaken identity he had been chased by the Mexican police from whom he had had to hide, and this caused a delay in his plans.

He told me this while serving me my breakfast late the following morning. I was far too discreet to press for further information, although on a subsequent occasion I suggested to him that he might make a little extra money writing for television.

During the five years that Albert was in my service in Pacific Palisades he must have become one of the richest men in the neighborhood. After he had encouraged me to lose a lot of weight while still extracting from me the same food allowance he got while he was fattening me up, he pointed out to me that my clothes no longer fitted me. It seemed only natural that I should give them to him, even though some of my suits were quite new. It would discourage me from putting on weight, Albert said, if I restricted myself to the use of the suits I had had cut to my new slender figure. I started to say something about having the old suits altered to fit me but the look in Albert's eye warned me to resist such bourgeois impulses.

Albert driving to the village supermarket in my Cadillac was a familiar sight in Pacific Palisades. In my well-tailored suits, his pockets bulging with my money, one of my best cigars jauntily clamped between his flashing white teeth, he made a profound impression upon the local inhabitants, who doffed their hats in awe and respect as he drove majestically by.

Yet it was Albert who played a very large part in making my bachelor life a happy one. The mere presence of another person somewhere in the house is all one needs to avoid loneliness.

I have found it quite impossible to sit down and read a

book in a completely empty house. Yet I have only to know that my servant is on his way back from the village with the groceries, and I feel perfectly relaxed and at ease. Man has solitary needs which can best be indulged when buttressed against the pressure of the herd.

There is no fun in being alone unless one can be alone against someone else. There is no point in having a den or sanctum sanctorum unless you can lock the door against at least one other person even if it is only your servant.

Albert was an excellent cook and knew how to do all the things around the house that wives do, except of course the only thing for which women are indispensable. But in regard to the latter the bachelor has no problems. On the contrary he has over the married man the not inconsiderable advantage of infinite variety.

Yet it is this very aspect of a bachelor's life that is usually his undoing, since he tends to have too many dates, and to regard his home as a sort of dressing room to be got in and out of as fast as he can change his clothes.

Once a man has acquired this habit pattern it will be intolerable for him to stay home at night and it will not be long therefore before he is caught by one of his dates and led resignedly to the altar, convinced that it is the only solution to his problem.

A bachelor should realize that all of the peacocking that goes on with his dates will be conspicuous by its absence once wedding bells have sounded its death knell. He will have to be prepared to face the truth of the old saying that the mat that says WELCOME when he is engaged, will say WIPE YOUR FEET when he is married.

The ashtray will no longer be pushed nearer to him as an act of simple solicitude but as a form of reprimand preceded by a purse-lipped look at the floor where he has dropped his ash.

A man must remember that good manners is an indulgence during courtship as opposed to a necessity in marriage. He will do well to remember the words of Congreve: "When we are married, let us be very strange and well-bred, as strange as if we had been married a very long time, and as well-bred as if we had never been married at all."

If the prospect of so much self-control fills him with dismay, then he may safely conclude that marriage is not for him.

He must then study the art of being a successful bachelor. One of the most valuable lessons he must learn in the process of becoming a highly skilled practitioner in this ancient though little understood art is not to try to score on the very first date he has with a prospective victim. To accomplish this and still have a well-rounded-out evening he can have a late date with a girl friend whom he has already broken in. In this manner he makes everybody happy while at the same time heightening the anticipation of things to come.

Tearing off a woman's clothes, or beating her into insensibility the first time you take her out to dinner is not generally speaking to be recommended as a form of initial approach, although it is rather frequently employed and very highly spoken of by some well-known bachelors, one of whom confided in me that he had to have it before dinner.

The real secret of success for a bachelor lies in staying at home most of the time and living the same sort of life he would lead if he were married to a *gemütliche* German *Hausfrau,* without being haunted by the appalling specter of eternal fidelity. He must make sure that his servant arranges flowers all over the house, puts mothballs in his closets, and generally speaking imitates to the best of his ability all of the captivating feminine touches with which a woman baits her trap.

If your servant can accomplish these things you can afford to turn a blind eye on his thefts and peccadilloes.

It is very important for a bachelor to live in a house that has no view, but rather looks out onto a garden full of trees which surround the house and protect him from the hostile world beyond.

A view tends to beckon to one and make one restless. Trees tend to soothe one and make one content to remain indoors. A view of the sea is all right until a ship appears on the horizon and one begins to wonder where it is going. A view of the city lights is positively dangerous, since it suggests night clubs and all the things a bachelor should try not to think about.

By learning to live alone in comfort a man can preserve his sovereign independence and enjoy his occasional picnics and parties, because the fun of such activities will be accentuated by the rich contrast they provide against the prosaic background of his normal life.

CHAPTER 5

THERE IS AN ENORMOUS ADVANTAGE to be gained from going to parties alone, particularly if one goes without a hat or coat. Upon entering the house and greeting the hostess with conventional gallantry one can give a quick glance round the room and size up the situation. The trained eye can tell at once if it promises to be a bore, and then while responding to the salutations of the guests with the required degree of affability one can work one's way to the bathroom, climb out of the window and drive home.

If you go to a party with the impedimenta of a date, an overcoat or a hat, you are sunk because then you have to leave by the front door and you are bound to be observed.

While it has been my misfortune to be placed in a position of having to resort to this stratagem on a number of occasions, I can quite confidently assure the reader that Hollywood parties by and large are the best in the world. The way the houses are designed and decorated in and around Beverly Hills and Bel Air is in itself an important factor in the making of a party. They are, generally speaking, newer, gayer, and, on account of the climate, cleaner than houses to be found elsewhere.

It was, of course, not always so. Twenty years ago the taste in houses and interior decoration in Hollywood was so deplorable as to stun the casual observer, while it mystified the conservative resident and provoked the sneers of visiting firemen.

But Hollywood has matriculated to a level of taste unequaled anywhere else in the world. Unhampered by tradition and enlightened through disastrous error and stalwart enterprise, her architects and designers have found unlimited scope for their talents because they have the backing of clients with imagination.

In other parts of the world it is still the old that commands respect and attention, while the new is consistently frowned upon. In Hollywood the reverse is the case. A house that is ten years old is considered unsafe to live in.

One of the few exceptions is Jack Warner's palace. It has stood as a monument to first-class architectual design for more than twenty-two years and is still the grandest and most elegant house in Hollywood. It is also still the scene of some of Hollywood's best parties.

Among houses with interesting architectual features is Greer Garson's in Bel Air. Her bathroom is done entirely in pink marble. The bath itself is of the sunken variety with great sea shells holding multicolored soaps and mysterious feminine paraphernalia. One side of the room is entirely of glass and opens onto a small and exotic garden which is completely walled-in and private so that one can walk about in the nude and take a sun bath. A long low garden chair rests among a profusion of gardenias and a great shining magnolia espaliered on the walls wafts its thick honeyed scent into the bathroom. This is probably the biggest production for the smallest audience yet to emerge from Hollywood.

One of Hollywood's best party-givers, director Jean Negulesco, has a large and comfortable establishment in the heart of Beverly Hills which houses two important collections. One is of the paintings of Bernard Buffet and the other is of his own waistcoats. He is as happy to show you the one as to wear the other and takes equal pride in both.

Jean makes a great host, partly because he is loaded with charm and partly because he is a terrific cook. At all of his parties he provides his guests with wild, unrecognizable Rumanian dishes so cunningly seasoned as to produce a sort of gastronomical conflagration. As strong drink is manifestly the only sensible remedy, the guests are very soon in an advanced state of high spirits and remain so until the early hours of the morning, by which time they are virtually indistinguishable from the gaunt gray masterpieces of Bernard Buffet that surround them on every side.

Joseph Cotten's house, hanging precariously from the cliffs of Santa Monica, sports two grand pianos, lofty rooms with frescoed ceilings, and an immense Palladian statue.

In Ronald Reagan's All-General-Electric house even the drinks seem to be served electronically.

One thinks also of the white and gold of Rosalind Russell's house as well as the ones with illuminated gardens and pools like Artur Rubinstein's which lend themselves so well to nocturnal festivities.

Hollywood hostesses go to endless pains to provide the best in food, entertainment, floral decorations, car-parking attendants, and bartenders who know how to keep the liquor flowing without the pauses that irritate their exacting guests.

Against this background the stars shine like the stars they are. Well turned out, done up to the teeth in the latest fashions, they are beautiful to behold.

At parties in the palace of Jack Warner there are always so many pretty girls that it is difficult not to gape.

One of Hollywood's indefatigable hostesses, Ouida Rathbone, upon receiving an acceptance note to an invitation she had issued, would call up the invited guest's wife and bully her into buying a new dress for the party. In this manner she would not only eliminate the doubt about what to wear that plagues all women, she would at the same time assure herself that the guests would come, and that they would be in the best possible mood for a party.

In the final analysis it is the guests that make the party, and how can you go wrong with the amount of talent constantly on tap in Hollywood?

I can remember a party at which the piano was successively occupied by Artur Rubinstein, Oscar Levant, and Cole Porter, while Danny Kaye clowned, and Judy Garland sang.

But while talent is also available in other cities as well as Hollywood, it is somehow not so easy to press into service elsewhere, perhaps because the general approach to parties in other places is more lukewarm, or perhaps because in Hollywood entertainers of all kinds feel more at home with one another in what to them is a sort of emotional native habitat. Whatever the cause, the effect is undeniable.

However, I must confess that in my own aging case these lighthearted festivities no longer have the same appeal they once had, partly because I am becoming increasingly absent-minded. While I was never very good at remembering names, the situation today is that I can scarcely remember my own. It is therefore in a state bordering on imbecilic befuddlement alternating with one of frozen terror that I approach the problem of introducing people, or of talking to people whose faces are the only things I know about them.

Actors generally stand about at parties waiting for people to come up and pay them compliments on their last performance. I saw Robert Mitchum, whom I both know and like, standing alone in such an attitude at a party once and I walked over to him with outstretched hand ready to exchange greetings and compliments. A moment before our hands met in a clasp that would have saved the evening, someone on my right slapped my shoulder and said hello to me. I responded in like measure and then turned back to Bob. I couldn't remember who he was. It had only been a moment's interruption but it was enough to upset the delicate mechanism of what I sometimes refer to rather facetiously as my brain.

"What I admire about you," I said expansively, covering the canvas of my inner turmoil with large brush strokes, "is your . . . your . . . well I mean your . . . what did you say your name was?"

Bob laughed heartily, evidently convinced that he had heard the expected compliment. "I would willingly exchange it for your . . . your . . . well I mean your . . . *je ne sais quoi,*" he said graciously, yet it seemed to me that he eyed me narrowly.

"*Je ne sais quoi,*" I muttered to myself uncomfortably—a pretty noncommittal phrase. Could it be that he too . . . ?

I was conscious of a sudden thirst and plunged gratefully into my whiskey and soda, retiring to fight again another day.

Coming up for air after a couple of deep restorative submersions I became somewhat myopically aware of a radiant apparition who seemed to be smiling at me through the mist of my tears. "How nice to see you" I said, straightening up with my very best social smile. "I have been looking for you all evening, Mrs. . . . er . . . Mrs. . . . silly of me," I said, snapping my fingers in frustration and speaking in the tone of one who has had a momentary lapse of memory. I looked at her expectantly. "I am Zsa Zsa," she said with tolerant amusement as she moved off in the direction of a room in which I presumed there must have been some hair dryers.

While I may have withdrawn with my tail between my legs from active participation in all but a few Hollywood parties, I am told they still go on with undiminished fervor. In any event, they will always remain in my memory as individual monuments to unfettered exuberance, endless generosity and fabulous faces, all of which, no doubt, have names.

It was at one of these Hollywood parties, as long ago as 1939, that I met a certain Benita Hume. She was evidently so impressed by my charm and good looks that she spared no effort to marry me off to an actress called Andrea Leeds. Devoted though she was to this scheme it failed as Miss Leeds very sensibly preferred to marry an enormously rich oil magnate.

The next time I met Miss Hume she had become Mrs. Ronald Colman and, undeterred by her previous failures, she once again sought to marry me off to a suitable lady of her acquaintance.

In the ensuing 20 years, whenever we happened to meet, she never failed to provide a matrimonial candidate for my perusal. Last year, however, after suffering her matchmaking for two decades, I put a permanent crimp in her plans. I reviewed her list of candidates and decided that the simplest plan of all would be for her to marry me herself. I suggested this somewhat radical solution to her on a couple of occasions without success. Persistence in the end paid off, however. Her hitherto unsuspected masochistic needs came to my assistance, and on the 10th of February, 1959, at three o'clock in the afternoon she drove with me to the British Consulate in Madrid where with a lamentable lack of self-control we were married.

On the whole I must say that I look upon Benita as the best thing that has happened in my life.

CHAPTER 6

I SIGNED FOR *Solomon and Sheba* in New York last August. I had just finished a picture with Sophia Loren at the old Movietone News Studios in Manhattan. I cannot remember what the story was about, I can only remember the heat. There was no air-conditioning in the studio and the heat was so great at times that one had to sit between scenes with ice cubes wrapped in towels pressed against all possible parts of the anatomy in order to survive.

It was a wonderful feeling to be whisked away from the heat of New York and to be dropped out of the sky, so to speak, into the coolness of London where everyone was, of course, complaining about the weather. I was "descended," as the French say, at my favorite London hotel where I was given a very elegant suite overlooking St. James's Park. Above the door there was a grille which had a small notice under it explaining somewhat gratuitously that it was a

143

ventilator, and that in order to operate it one had only to pull the chain. The chain was missing.

As I went into the bathroom to shave I felt a little sad about not being able to use my American electric shaver, London current being 230 volts. I had bought an ordinary safety razor and was not looking forward to the nicks and scratches with which my face would soon be adorned. Imagine my delight when I found that the hotel had installed a voltage transformer making it possible to use my shaver. I was deliriously happy. The fact that it was temporarily out of order did not dampen my spirits in the least. To get on the phone to the desk was for me the work of a moment. The management assured me that the gadget would be repaired as soon as the man who attended to that sort of thing returned from his annual vacation in two weeks' time. They said that there were several repair jobs on the list ahead of mine, but there was always the chance that they might have some cancellation, in which case they would be able to improve my priority. I felt it would be churlish of me to inquire whether there might be someone else in London with the necessary skill to effect at least a temporary repair job, so I let the matter drop and reconciled myself to shaving with my safety razor. I was to be in London at least three weeks doing costume fittings for the picture, consequently the last week could be looked forward to as "uncut-face week." As the management had been so exceedingly cooperative in regard to the promise of a repair job on my voltage transformer, I felt it imprudent to mention the fact that my john was out of order. There would be plenty of time to sit on the john in Spain which is in any case the principal activity of the tourist.

My stay in England came to an end all too soon. The weather, that most thrilling of subjects for English residents, had been in my solitary opinion delightful.

I saw some stimulating theatrical productions and renewed old friendships in London wherein my stay was agreeably punctuated by weekends in Kent, whose luminescent countryside beckons to me still.

I took the "gourmet" flight to Paris for one of my weekends and was again amazed by the shortness of the trip as well as by the indefatigable efforts of the stewards and hostesses to press drinks upon me and stuff food into my mouth from take-off to touch-down. When I entered the airport building at Le Bourget and reached for my passport, my hand closed upon a sandwich which the thoughtful hostess must have slipped into my pocket to allay any pangs of hunger I might still have. When I was asked in Customs if I had anything to declare, my reply was unintelligible because my mouth was still full of cake.

The formalities over, I made a muck of climbing into a cab outside the building and the kindly, understanding driver gave me a helping hand as I staggered for a moment on the pavement. He settled me back into the seat and wiped off the brandy that was oozing out of my ears.

Paris is a different place everytime you go to it, mainly because it does not change. You change, and blame it on Paris.

On this occasion it welcomed me with the open arms of glorious weather which I made the most of by doing something I had never done before. I took a ride up the Seine in a *bâteau mouche*. It was a perfectly delightful experience although it would certainly never have occurred to me to spend any time in this manner on previous visits. I had thought of Paris in terms of its restaurants and the night life of Montmartre which used to have an appeal for me on previous visits. I now saw a new Paris whose existence I had only vaguely suspected and I sat quite entranced with my discovery as I watched it glide by me in the afternoon sun. The fine old hotel overlooking the Place Vendome where I stayed had on exhibition the same octogenarian ladies drinking tea in the palm court that I had seen in earlier years looking no younger, and I found their longevity heartening.

While taking a walk in the gardens of the Luxembourg Palace I ran into the usual black market money-changer lurking behind a fountain.

Although for a moment I was tempted, I resisted his importunities with commendable hauteur and congratulated myself later on having done so, for in discussing the matter with the concierge of the hotel I was informed by that omniscient being that these shady characters, whom he felt he should not even soil his mouth by mentioning, not only gave you counterfeit money, they even short-changed you in that. Though whether you are worse off in having nine thousand forged francs than you are in having ten thousand forged francs is an interesting field for speculation. However, I adopted what I felt was a suitable air of shocked surprise at this piece of information and entrusted the changing of my money to the concierge. It seemed to me that he counted it out very quickly but I decided not to double check it because I preferred not to run the risk of having my abiding faith in human nature shaken any more than was necessary.

Qn the day that I left Paris I was in something of a hurry and packed my bag rather quickly, having first rung the bell for the maid to whom I was going to give the usual tip. No one answered the bell in the interval between the time I rang it and the time I finished packing and I concluded that perhaps as it was still early morning there just wasn't anyone up and about. I opened the door and looked down the corridor. The entire hotel staff was there, skillfully deployed, in extended formation, standing at attention and looking me straight in the eye.

"American tourists must have been responsible for this deplorable state of affairs," I muttered to myself as I distributed largesse left and right.

It was a relief to board a London-bound plane where no matter how much they might stuff me with food, at least I would not have to shell out any more tips.

My stay in London was coming to an end. It was already September, and the fifteenth of the month—the day I was to start shooting *Solomon and Sheba* in Spain—suddenly loomed into view and I was whisked off to Madrid and thence to Zaragoza where I was "descended" at the Grand Hotel and accommodated in a very pleasant though small suite whose bathroom—the focal point of my interest—sported to my enormous and immediate relief a toilet of unexampled efficiency.

The location where we were going to shoot the exteriors of the picture was the Spanish military encampment of Valdespartera, a vast open plain some fifteen minutes' drive out of Zaragoza. It was said that during the civil war a total of 12,000 people were murdered there, presumably marched out of the city and machine-gunned, their money and property having been seized. The people of Zaragoza are still rather bitter about it; consequently we were in a somewhat delicate position in view of the fact that we were proposing to tramp about on what was virtually hallowed ground.

But the encampment suited our purposes perfectly, and it was certainly the most comfortable and best organized location I have ever been on. The various military buildings that bordered the plain were taken over by the company and transformed into make-up department, wardrobe, property room and mess room or commissary. The latter was not only a large, comfortable whitewashed room but the food was without a doubt the best ever served on location, a fact which soon became known in the town and consequently an invitation to lunch at the commissary became a highly cherished privilege.

The lunches were of four courses served with wines and finished off with brandy, and were of a quality quite unheard of in the business. The battle scenes employed a total of some three thousand Spanish soldiers and called for masterly organization. They all had to be provided with spears, shields, costumes, chariots, bows and arrows and food.

When we were actually joined in battle it was quite terrifying. Even though they were only mock battles, they might almost as well have been in earnest if we consider the amount of damage and the number of casualties involved. No less than twelve horses were killed and countless extras were carted off to the hospital with broken ankles, broken collarbones, or just plain exhaustion and shock. It was nothing short of a miracle that no human lives were lost, and there were times when I seriously doubted my own chances of survival.

I cannot say that I acquitted myself nobly on the field of battle. My sword was made of rubber, my shield of Fiberglas, my breastplate of lightweight papier mâché. All I had to do was to look heroic and not fall out of my chariot. I was hard put to it to do either. To look heroic when one is terrified is no easily accomplished feat. If I had fallen backwards out of my chariot I would have been trampled to death by the horses drawing the chariot behind me. We were galloping at breakneck speed over rough terrain and I had only a small concealed leather strap to hang on to with my left hand while I was brandishing my broadsword with my right. How those fellows managed to do it for real in days of old, weighted down with the authentic metal armor, is something that is quite beyond my limited powers of comprehension. As it was I ended up each day a mass of scratches and bruises just from bumping against the sides and front of the chariot, in spite of the fact that all possible inside surfaces had been lined with sponge rubber by the thoughtful property department in order to give me the maximum possible protection.

To add to my discomfort I was, of course, suffering from the sort of upset stomach that plagues most foreigners in Spain, and certainly all of those who venture anywhere near Zaragoza where the water is perpetually contaminated.

A combination of abject terror and upset stomach does not, generally speaking, contribute much to the kind of mood that is needed for an actor to envisage a heroic playing attitude.

The plain of Valdespartera was covered with a dust surface as fine as ash. It would billow out from behind our wheels like smoke.

One of the shots we made called for the foot soldiers to run diagonally across the path of the charging chariots. Because of the dust we raised they could not see us very well, nor we them. We passed right over one young man who was unaware of our proximity and, therefore, did not leap aside in time. Our horses clubbed him down with their hoofs and our chariot did the rest. My chariot driver did not even see him, so intent was he upon controlling our frightened horses in our wild stampede.

I turned aghast and strained my eyes to look through the billowing dust we were raising at the crumpled and inert figure we had left in our wake. I heard the voice of a Spanish officer shouting to him to get up and run or he would spoil the shot. He was only a boy of nineteen or so doing what was supposed to be his military service, and he did his best to respond. I saw him stagger to his feet, walk a few steps, and then go down for good. An ambulance collected him soon afterwards and carted him off to the hospital. We heard that he survived all right, so he must have been made of stern stuff.

The co-operation of the Spanish authorities as well as the willingness of the men to expose themselves to danger and hardship was truly exemplary. If production has largely moved away from Hollywood, it is becoming more and more obvious why. The kind of scenes we shot in Zaragoza can no longer be filmed in Hollywood because apart from the colossal difference in cost, the extras would not be willing to endure the discipline and hardships attendant upon such endeavors. It is easier for them to draw unemployment insurance.

The man who complained least about our hardships was Tyrone Power, who seemed to be having the time of his life and set an example for all of cheerful fortitude.

Yet, for all his popularity, Tyrone's presence in Zaragoza did not create the stir that was brought about by the arrival of Gina Lollobrigida.

It is the custom in Zaragoza, as indeed it is in all Spanish towns and villages, for virtually the entire population to go strolling between the hours of seven and nine in the evening up and down the main *paseo*. It is a practical idea as it provides the men with the chance to look all the girls over without being plagued by the gnawing fear that somewhere, in some kitchen or attic, there is a madly attractive Cinderella whom they are destined never to meet.

On the evening of Gina Lollobrigida's arrival an unprecedented change in this age-old and deeply revered custom took place.

The entire route of the strolling oglers was changed to encompass the Grand Hotel, which was a full two blocks away from the main *paseo*.

The crowds never got to see Gina except for a fleeting glimpse or two when she ran from the car up the steps of the hotel. The roar they would let out then was blood-curdling. It sounded like a hundred thousand hungry lions in good voice, and it would cause me to hide under the covers of my bed, teeth chattering like a frozen monkey.

Some twelve miles out of Zaragoza there is an American Air Force base to which we were invited from time to time by the base commander, Colonel Preston, and where we gave a concert on the last Saturday night of our stay in Zaragoza.

The concert was an impromptu affair in which Tyrone was the main attraction and the solid part of the show. He gave a ten-minute reading from Thomas Wolfe. It was very effective and afterwards I persuaded him to memorize the whole thing so that he could do it again at the big Torejon air base near Madrid. Effective as his reading was I felt it would be a hundred times more so if he could do it without the book. He agreed with me and set himself to work on the not inconsiderable task of committing to memory a whole chapter of involved prose. It was a feat I would never have had the gumption to attempt. Three days later he made his appearance at the air base in circumstances somewhat different from those we had planned.

The concert in Zaragoza was a great success not so much because of what we did, but because of the relaxed atmosphere we created in advance.

Ted Richmond, our producer, made an excellent M.C., being a natural ad-lib artist. I played the piano and sang a couple of songs, and Tyrone did his reading. I finished on the wrong note to the kind of tumultuous applause a Metropolitan opera star has to rupture himself to get. I shudder to think of the sort of reception a paying audience would have accorded my performance.

As it was we left Zaragoza in a blaze of glory, having successfully completed all of our battle scenes and having done our bit toward lightening the burden of the Air Force boys' tour of duty, their grateful applause still rang in our ears as we turned the noses of our cars in the direction of Madrid and stepped on the gas.

The first thing I did upon arrival in the metropolis was to go to the Ritz Hotel and try to talk them into letting me have a suite. I entered this venerable establishment somewhat timorously for I had heard that they had made a hard and fast rule against accommodating members of our profession. I was told that this rule had been made after Victor Mature had bestowed the somewhat hard-to-appraise benefits of his patronage upon the hotel. He had apparently shown such liberal signs of *joie-de-vivre* that he not only got himself thrown out but brought into being the unofficial—almost furtive—ban against all actors.

As I tiptoed through the revolving doors and approached the reception desk, I became instantly aware of the glacial atmosphere that pervaded the lobby. The reception clerk greeted me with a lateral movement of the lips conveying recognition, understanding, and rejection; but which was in no circumstances to be confused with a smile.

"Yes, Mr. Sanders?" he said, rather kindly I thought. "What can I do for you?"

I was a little bit encouraged by the tone of his voice and so I managed to stop fidgeting with my hat and umbrella as I shuffled closer with a view to bringing about a conspiratorial rapport with the man.

"I . . . er . . . I er . . . I . . . er . . . I . . . er I," I said, unable yet to control my trembling lips and tongue that had grown too big for my mouth.

"A reservation?" said the clerk, unexpectedly helpful.

"Ye-ye-ye-ye-yes blease," I managed to say with a sort of German accent.

"When would you like it?" asked the clerk.

I was gaining confidence. "As soon as possible," I enunciated clearly.

The clerk began to study a book that lay in front of him on the desk, while I turned to survey the lobby, and, beyond it, the main public rooms of what I felt was soon to become my home.

There was no sign of life anywhere. The place seemed to be deserted, nothing moved, no one came in or went out. It could have been an abandoned hotel in some mining ghost town in the Far West. The only sound disturbing the eerie stillness was made by the clerk as he turned the apparently blank pages of the book he was studying.

At length he looked up at me with a disarming smile.

"We have a small room in the annex which has a washbasin—the bathroom is on the lower floor," he said.

"When can I have it?" I demanded excitedly even though I knew I didn't want it.

"It will be available in January, 1973," he said, looking me straight in the eye.

"Book it for me," I said unflinchingly.

I held his look until my eyes began to water and then I turned and handed my hat and umbrella to a solicitous page boy and made my way toward the Palm Court, and thence to the dining room where I was greeted by the strains of the lunchtime orchestra which was playing "Fascination" to an audience of yawning waiters and an empty room. The maître d'hôtel hurried forward mammoth menu in hand.

"Just one." I said laconically, and stopped to give him time to ponder the problem while I gazed round the room. The maître d' seemed to be momentarily nonplused by the wealth of opportunity he was able to offer his solitary patron, but eventually he made up his mind and led me to a table by the window where I was immediately surrounded by solicitous waiters glad to have something to do for a change.

The orchestra rather appropriately started playing "Just One of Those Things," and after listening to their rendition for a while I understood why the waiters had been yawning, and I began to yawn too. However, I checked myself quickly as I did not want to give the hotel authorities an opportunity to criticize my manners and on that account cancel my reservation. I screwed my monocle into my eye and crooked my little finger as I raised my coffee cup to my lips. I discreetly applauded when the orchestra finished its piece. The *chef d'orchestra* looked at me with amazement, but I held my ground and smiled appreciatively. I made a friend for life.

But it was time for me to be getting back to the Castellana Hilton where the free souls of this world are more easily tolerated than at the Ritz. I had to consolidate my immediate position there and did not feel any too secure about it as I had heard that Ava Gardner had just been thrown out of it—a distinction of a much higher order of magnitude than that achieved by Victor Mature.

Incidentally, Zsa Zsa beat everyone at this game when she succeeded in getting herself thrown out of jail, which takes a bit of doing. She was arrested for speeding in Santa Barbara and a rather poor view was taken of her truculent attitude by the arresting officer, who forthwith carted her off to the cooler where she put on a scene of such majestic proportions as quite pulverized the police force, who insisted that they were running a respectable jail and were unaccustomed to such highly colored coherence. They threw her out with the greatest indignation. Having been myself thrown out of so many jobs, shows, and countries—although not yet hotels —I view the whole thing with sympathetic interest.

In Hollywood, for instance, arrangements of the golf clubs are such as to make the atmosphere of exclusion a chronic condition. There are clubs into which you can't get if you are a Christian, others if you are a Jew, and others if you are an actor. The ones into which anyone can get are of course unsuccessful and empty.

I was turning such morbid thoughts over in my mind as I left the Ritz, and with a view to achieving a certain mental prophylaxis I decided to drop into the world-famous Prado museum which is virtually next door.

I should not want it thought that I have anything but wholehearted enthusiasm, respect and veneration for culture. I am deeply in favor of any aspect of culture and any aspect of art.

Yet I sometimes feel puzzled. Once in a while I have an uneasy qualm that I should know more about painting in order to understand more; there is doubt in my mind as to the exact meaning of a masterpiece. I feel the finer points are passing me by. Well, what I am really wondering is why the goddam thing was painted in the first place and who had a sense of humor warped enough to suggest hanging it.

The Prado is supposed to house one of the world's great collection of pictures. One of the first questions asked of a foreigner in Madrid is whether he has been to the Prado. Natives as well as tourists who have been to it manage to pronounce the word Prado with a tone of hushed awe which seems to put a sort of halo around it.

The experts speak just as reverently as the laymen about the wonders contained in this great museum and I am more than willing to bow to their superior knowledge—since the lighting is arranged in such a way as to make it virtually impossible to see more than a very small portion of any given painting and one is, therefore, in no position to produce any valid opinion to the contrary.

You come in first to a circular room sparsely hung with some very fine *"paintings by* PEETER SNAYERS (1592-1666) *of the arrival of the Infanta Isabel Clara Eugenia in Breda, and the Rescue of Leride in 1646."* One feels a faint desire for an aqua lung as the atmosphere and lighting in the room have a rather submarine tinge. You advance then to a gallery about as long as Piccadilly, and if the sun happens to be in the right position you will receive the full force of such a succession of bleeding wounds, bulging eyeballs, twisted sinews, crucifixions, as would keep the Marquis de Sade agog for a month of Sundays.

One cannot help speculating as to whether painting subjects of such excessive discomfort with such barefaced gusto does not indicate a rather curious attitude toward life and one not usually encouraged by the official guardians of public morality.

There is one picture in particular on which I would appreciate some outside views. I mention it in no spirit of criticism, but just as a matter of simple inquiry. I am a student of life and anxious only to learn.

It is a sizable canvas by Peter Paul Rubens called "The God Saturn." It shows a rather large man whose hair is soft and wavy. He is bending over a baby which he holds carefully in his delicately drawn hands. He is in fact eating the baby, who, understandably, is taking it in very bad part and holds its mouth open in an expression of high-spirited protest. The colors and method of painting in this in no way match the astonishing subject, that is to say they are neither violent nor angular. On the contrary, the lines are soft and rounded and the colors mellow.

Now, all I would like to know is, does one actually enjoy the idea of a man occupied in eating a baby as the subject of a painting? Is one stimulated by the subject under any circumstances? To get right down to it, who needs it?

Much as I hunger for enlightenment and welcome instruction, I feel one should be selective as to its source. I am thinking of the astounding dissemination not of knowledge but of arbitrary taste and opinion emanating constantly from a powerful group known as "they." This group exercises its pressure mainly upon women who are inclined to rule their lives by what "they" say. One might reasonably conclude that women have practically thrown over "theism" in exchange for "theyism." If everyone suddenly decides to appear with tilted eyes or feels that it is necessary to live on yogurt or to listen to Mozart at Glyndebourne, the sinister shadow of "they" may be glimpsed lurking in the background. One sees its influence upon the hosts of tourists that pound their way indefatigably through cathedrals. In years gone by I might have been prepared to wager that cathedrals would never replace the movies in popularity, but with the rising power of "theyism" I am no longer so confident. There may be several good reasons for visiting a cathedral. I may in time discover some for myself. As far as I am concerned "they" can save their breath to cool their porridge.

Shooting in Madrid had started with interior scenes in which Tyrone and Gina were supposed to engage in some horseplay and which did not concern me, so I had a little time to write some more chapters for this book and do some sight-seeing.

Driving around Madrid and its environs, one is impressed by the refreshing absence of billboards. For me it was quite a new experience to drive out into the country and see the road stretch ahead through fields and woods unencumbered by instructions on how I should brush my teeth or what I should drink.

Spain is a poor country. One might say that it is too poor to enjoy the luxury of bad taste.

Of course, it must be said in defense of billboards that there are parts of Los Angeles that are so ugly as to be actually improved by them.

Advertising in America is governed by a policy of national saturation and since billboards are so colorful, massive and numerous, most communities lie more or less entirely concealed behind this vital aspect of American life. From every side, on boardings and walls, great vistas of mountains and lakes catch the eye, and while the beholder rejoices in the panorama he is refreshed by the thought of the beer it praises, although he may find the connection a tenuous one, as indeed I do myself.

Mr. Jantzen's sumptuous bathing costumes give graphic proof that the longest curve between two points has more to be said for it than the straight line the mathematicians are so keen on.

The Cemeteries combine, with laudable yet alarming candor, the melancholy nape of a neck, a glistening statue and the reasonable price of eternity.

Behind all this eclectic art and gratuitous information cowers the city. In the case of Los Angeles the results of the efforts of the city fathers, architects and real estate tycoons have been so disastrous as to make the billboard overgrowth an unqualified success. It climbs, one might say if one were given to hyperbole, like a multicolored vine over the chaotic tumble of bricks and mortar which is called with such reckless abandon, the City of the Angels.

Madrid has no such protective covering, and needs none. Every intersection glitters with great fountains, and the blazing sun is filtered everywhere by lines of immaculately kept trees beneath which the populace disports itself, strolling, sitting or passing the time of day at the outdoor cafés and observing the astounding tactics of the local taxi drivers, whose homicidal predelictions match, if not surpass, those of the French.

Flowers are everywhere; El Retiro Park is probably the most spectacular in Europe. Here statuary is absolutely rampant and if it gives the impression sometimes of being wrought out of marzipan, still it has its own quality of splendor if only by nature of its abundance.

As an added charm the officials of the gardens are all decked out in nut-brown and orange crowned with very rakish hats, and one feels they might well burst into an aria at any moment. I have even considered approaching one of them concerning the possibilities of a duet. At the gateways old ladies sit tented in faded black cloaks and topped by a crowd of multicolored balloons which give their ancient faces an incongruous air of hilarity.

The whole city is full of ornate buildings, tremendous iron doorways, fine vistas and wide skyscapes, and lies on its mesa like a Christmas decoration dropped on the bare moon-like terrain around it.

The custom so jealously preserved by Spaniards of taking two and a half hours off for lunch every day was hard for us to get accustomed to, and, in fact, on the picture we stuck to the normal one-hour lunch break.

The picture had been moving along without incident. There was the usual horseplay, and the schedule was comfortable.

Our distinguished director, King Vidor, guided us gently through our paces and gave generously of his vast store of artistic wisdom. (It is a matter of business principle with me to treat directors with craven servility.)

I have never felt more highly complimented than when a member of a group of visiting American tourists came up to me on the set, and surveying me in my regal costume, asked me if it was true that I was playing the part of King Vidor.

There was nothing in those early days to warn us of the impending tragedy that was to have such a profound effect upon our carefree lives.

CHAPTER 7

Till man's last day is come we should not dare,
Of happiness to say what was his share,
For of no man can it be truly said,
That he is happy till he first be dead.
                                        —Ovid

SATURDAY THE FIFTEENTH of November
was just another day in our lives. The picture was more or
less on schedule. The producers seemed to be satisfied with
the results of our work. Everyone was in good health and
high spirits and looking forward to some fun and games
over the weekend.

The day's shooting call included Tyrone Power, myself,
and our two doubles. The scene to be shot was the final
duel in the picture in which I was to die.

161

Everybody was on time in the morning. Tyrone and I rehearsed the scene and then went back to our dressing-room-trailers while the cameraman and his assistants lighted the set. We had a brief but animated discussion about our plans to settle in Switzerland. Tyrone was glowing with enthusiasm over the prospect. Somebody came up to us and broke up our discussion and Tyrone wandered off toward his trailer and I made for mine.

Presently the assistant director came to see me and told me that I could relax, that we would not be shooting the scene for a little while because Tyrone had had some kind of spasm.

I remembered that he had said something about having a touch of bursitis and assumed that it had kicked up again. I wandered over to his trailer and opened the door. He was sitting in a chair twisted over on his left side and holding on tightly to his arm. His head was tilted over rigidly as though some crick in his neck prevented him from straightening it. Even though he was wearing make-up his face had a sort of bluish color, but he greeted me with a smile.

"What's up?" I said.

"Oh, it'll go away," he said, "I've had it before. It's this damned bursitis."

I suggested to him that he should lie down but he said it felt worse when he tried to stretch out.

Our producer, Ted Richmond, long-time friend of Tyrone's came in at this point looking very worried. I had a feeling that they wanted to be alone so I discreetly closed the door and went back to my trailer. I am abysmally ignorant in medical matters, and was quite sure that in a few moments Tyrone would be all right and that we would do the scene as planned.

I began reading a magazine and did not notice the passage of time. There came a knock on my door and the assistant director poked his head in and told me that shooting had been called off for the day. It was a Saturday and I was delighted. It would give me a longer weekend. The assistant director looked at me. "I suppose you know that Tyrone died," he said. "Don't be an ass," I laughed. Then I noticed the expression on the man's face. "You're joking," I said. "It would be a pretty poor joke if I were," he said soberly, and we began to stare at one another.

The situation was quite incomprehensible to me. I walked toward the make-up department trying to understand it. Members of the company were grouped together in clusters, their faces betraying utter bewilderment and frozen disbelief. Mechanically I changed my clothes and drove back to the hotel, where I saw Ted Richmond and Debbie Power standing in the doorway. They must have been on their way to the morgue. Their faces looked as if they were made of stone.

I was almost overwhelmed by a feeling of incredulity. I was quite sure that there had been some fantastic mistake; that Tyrone would show up again and that we would have a good laugh about it.

Later on I spent some time with Debbie Power. Like the rest of us I had grown very fond of her. Her infectious humor had illuminated our frequent meetings. She had been the life and soul of the many parties we had had. She was a gay companion for Tyrone. She was all shot to pieces but she was bearing up courageously. She too had the feeling that he would walk into the room at any moment. She too was bewildered.

During the days that followed I had ample time to reflect upon the extraordinary enigma of death.

Tyrone Power was so young, so strong, so full of life, so full of plans for the future. How could so much energy suddenly evaporate? And where did it all go?

Man's deep-seated need for an answer to this sort of question has kept the organized Church perpetually occupied in attempting to supply it. But just how satisfactory is the Church's answer when one comes face to face with the question? I must confess that in this particular case the answer only served to increase my bewilderment.

A few days after Tyrone died his body was flown to Hollywood where a funeral service was held in the Chapel of the Psalms. The nature of the ceremony, and the behavior of the people attending it, have come in for a good deal of criticism, yet I must say that from my point of view nothing that happened could have been any stranger than the event itself.

The fact that the organ played Irving Berlin's "I'll Be Loving You Always" at the service struck many people as being inappropriate to the occasion. But to me it would have been just as inappropriate if conventional psalms and hymns had been played. Whatever songs are sung, whatever music is played, whatever rituals are performed, they do not to my way of thinking restore the loss, express the grief, or even dignify the occasion.

The professional mourners of Dickensian England, the black-plumed horses of France, the uproarious Irish wakes, the Indian suttee, are surely only manifestations of the strange fact that death seems to bring out in man an instinct for festival.

As they no doubt did at the funerals of Hadrian, of Caligula, and of Tutankamen, the crowd outside the Chapel of the Psalms had brought box lunches, bawling babies, and hula hoops. The arrival of each of the guests was greeted by the crowd with bursts of applause that varied in intensity with the importance of the guest. Loud cheers announced the arrival of Yul Brynner. It was as though by replacing

Tyrone in the picture, he was somehow making everything all right.

At one point the behavior of the public became so unruly that the police were obliged to put into effect Riot Procedure Number 3, whereby they control the crowd by simply riding into it in a phalanx.

The exhausts of their motorcycles shattered the air, drowning out Cesar Romero who was speaking the eulogy, jarring the sentimental strains of the organ, but somehow failing to ruffle the calm of a strange oriental woman in full Chinese costume who had been standing in a sort of trance by the coffin during this portion of the service. It was later revealed that the oriental woman was none other than Miss Loretta Young who had come straight from the set of a TV show.

If one should get the feeling that such goings on were a trifle grotesque, let us consider the events that took place in the supposedly more orthodox atmosphere of somber, Catholic Spain.

A burial mass was said for Tyrone Power at the Church of San Francisco el Grande. Cards were passed out at the entrance to the church, both in English and in Spanish, which read as follows:

One of the greatest tributes paid to Tyrone Power was by a friend of many years' standing.

Before leaving Madrid, Mrs. Power expressed a wish that the many individuals involved in the production *Solomon and Sheba* and Mr. Power's friends be given an opportunity to read the following tribute to the actor by Mr. George Sanders.

I shall always remember Tyrone Power as a bountiful man. A man who gave freely of himself. It mattered not to whom he gave. His concern was in the giving. I shall always remember his wonderful smile, a smile that would light up the darkest hour of the day like a sunburst.

I shall always remember Tyrone Power as a man who gave more of himself than it was wise for him to give. Until in the end he gave his life.

This little eulogy, though perhaps falling short of full justice to the subject, was nevertheless the only means by which we were able to relate the events that followed with the memory of the man whose loss we were mourning.

It was the only mention made of the deceased's name at any time during the service. I am fully aware of the great comfort and solace that the organized Church brings to its millions of devout supporters. I know that prayer is highly esteemed by those who have a deep-seated need for its therapy. I know that one must, at the very least, pay lip service to the Church's concept of immortality or suffer the dire consequences of a loss of respect for human life.

Yet I am bewildered by the mumbo-jumbo of church rituals. I am not irreligious, atheistic or irreverent. I am not a champion of apostasy nor even an agnostic. I am just plain bewildered.

I found it difficult to understand why the priest kept talking Latin all the time, a language which after all is not among the most popular.

It was a very large church and the altar was situated at a distance of some hundred yards or so from the main body of the building where the congregation was deployed. We did not come equipped with binoculars, consequently it was with some difficulty that we were able to tell whether anything was really going on back there.

The priest remained at the altar throughout the ceremony, performing rituals that were as arcane as they were indiscernible.

At his feet, like a couple of playful spaniels, were the thoroughly seedy-looking altar boys, with dirty white surplices and grubby hands. One of them had a large, bronze hand bell which he would ring from time to time. This appeared to be a signal for us to stand if we were sitting or to sit if we were standing. Once in a while he would give the bell a double clang, which meant that we were to give up whatever we were doing and kneel.

I strongly suspected the boy of ringing the bell more often than was necessary. I thought he had a rather spiteful look on his pimply face and that his attitude was out of keeping with the solemnity of the occasion.

At all events we did our best to follow his signals. However, not being Catholics, none of us had had any prior indoctrination into this type of ceremonial punctilio, and I am afraid that we never got any of it right.

I often wonder whether a feeling I sometimes experience is shared by others when they find themselves in similar circumstances, or whether it is peculiar to me and consequently psychopathological.

If I look down from the top of a tall building and watch the antlike traffic in the streets below, I am conscious of a morbid urge to throw myself out of the window, and I shrink back in horror, not so much at the thought of it as at the thought of having had the thought.

If I find myself in a church or cathedral or in any large gathering place where people have assembled to observe a solemn occasion, I am conscious then, too, of a morbid urge to cry out or make a rude noise or to start singing a song.

I had such a feeling at the burial mass. It was aggravated to no small extent by the gymnastics we were called upon to perform and by the fact that two Spanish press photographers —one on either side of the center aisle—were snapping pictures of us incessantly throughout the service. They almost blinded us with their flash bulbs and we were very angry with them. Since I was sitting in the front pew, the photographer on my side was quite close to me. He seemed to be taking a sadistic delight in my discomfort. He wore a supercilious smirk that would broaden into a grin every time I got up or sat down.

There was nothing very much I could do about him during the service, but I made up my mind to give him a severe reprimand as soon as we were out of the church. I sized him up. He was not as tall as I am but he was stocky and he was younger. Still, I thought I could take him on if necessary. I felt I could level with him all right.

Toward the end of the service the priest wandered off to the side and changed his suit or whatever it was that he had on. He needn't have bothered. He looked about the same when he came back. But it was a welcome diversion. One which I hoped would lead up to an interesting spectacle of some kind. But in this I was disappointed. The ceremony came to an end as colorlessly as it had begun.

The priest and the altar boys drifted silently around the altar and disappeared through some concealed exit like so much cigarette smoke wafted through an opened window. The congregation began to shuffle out of the church, and in a trance of imbecilic bewilderment, I followed.

At the door of the church I came face to face with my press photographer. He was looking at me with a fatuous grin. Butterflies crowded into my stomach. For a moment I was tempted to pretend to myself that I had made no decision to put things to rights with this young man. On the other hand, I had to live with myself.

So I quelled my misgivings and faced him with a hostile glare. Perhaps the reader will best catch the mood of the dialogue that followed if I translate it literally from the Spanish.

"You have been making to me the cuff," I said to the photographer in a harsh, accusatory tone.

He was visibly taken aback by this and I thought he looked rather guilty.

"Since later it makes fault to me to tell you that are a without shame you," I said, following up my advantage.

"But, señor," he said.

"Oh, go yourself to the whore-mother who bore you," I said, delivering the supreme insult.

For a moment his eyes glittered and a murderous look came over his swarthy face. He took a step toward me and then just as quickly stopped as a look of infinite compassion suffused his features.

"Señor," he said, "it makes grace to me that you should say that. You do not give to yourself account of what has passed to you. It is to you the fly-buttons are undone."

I was not to be so easily taken in.

"It is to me the hair you are taking," I replied, guardedly.

"Then look," he said.

I looked. He was right.

"You have reason," I said, with a high-pitched, hysterical giggle as I adjusted my dress.

I did a sort of Jack Buchanan soft-shoe time step to cover my embarrassment and lurched out of the place, missing my footing on one of the steps leading down to the street.

There was a sort of commissionaire fellow that the Studio had laid on to control the crowd outside the church. He caught me in his arms like a football.

"A taxi, Don Jorge?" he inquired solicitously.

"Yes, by favor," I replied. "A taxi!"

As I was being driven away to resume the sometimes chaotic, sometimes gay, but always interesting life of which Tyrone had become so much a part, I again began to feel the burden of his loss. It was a loss that with the passage of time would be less keenly felt although ineluctably present. It was a loss that was essentially ours; in no way his. Tyrone died in possession of all his faculties, at the height of his powers, and in the full bloom of his manhood. It would not be incongruous to say that he died bursting with health.

Those of us who must look forward to advancing decrepitude may think of him at times with a certain degree of envy. For while ours was the loss, who knows but what his was the gain.

> Whom the gods love die young; that man is blest
> Who having viewed at ease this solemn show
> Of sun, stars, ocean, fire, doth quickly go
> Back to his home with calm uninjured breast.
> Be life or short or long, 'tis manifest
> Thou ne'er wilt see things goodlier, Parmeno,
> Than these; then take thy sojourn here as though
> Thou wert some playgoer or wedding-guest
> The sooner sped the safelier to thy rest,
> Well-furnished, foe to none, with strength at need,
> Shalt thou return; while he who tarries late,
> Faints on the road wornout, with age oppressed
> Harassed by foes whom life's dull tumults breed
> Thus ill dies he for whom death long doth wait.

CHAPTER **8**

To the englishman it is a continual source of amazement and irritation that the rest of mankind does not consist of other Englishmen. To him the world is full of foreigners—strange backward peoples who have inexplicably failed to master the English tongue.

Though I am a somewhat hybrid Englishman I have something of this national trait in me. I tend to consider anyone who does not speak my language as barbaric, uneducated and unsporting. On this basis, if on no other, the Japanese must rank as one of the most uncivilized nations in the world. I was in Japan early this year making a film. The story was about the sinking of an ocean liner. It was to be called *The Last Voyage,* and as far as I can gather the only reason we went to Japan to make it was because Japanese ship-breakers had bought the *Ile de France* and—for $4000 a day—were prepared to let us help break it up.

Having been assured by our Swiss friends—none of whom had any intention of going there—that Japan was absolute heaven we set off stoically guzzling champagne.

At Cairo they were eager for all sorts of written assurances and personal news as to one's name, age, financial prospects and how and who were one's grandparents. I thought it a rather touching sign of their personal regard; especially as the plane only stayed for 30 minutes. At Calcutta and Bangkok we didn't get out in case they would want to fingerprint us. Eventually the Swissair plane floated us into the pouring rain of Tokyo's airport. We waded ashore and looked around us, soaking up the soaking atmosphere of the Far East.

It was interesting, if a little surprising, to see an American involved in considerable troubles because he did not have a visa. I say surprising, because although by now one is perfectly accustomed to the fact that the fruits of victory have been changed somewhere along the line to hot potatoes, still one would like to think there might remain, if not fruits, at least some not inconsiderable pip. Like, say, not requiring a visa for the victor to visit the vanquished.

It is well known however that one of the great preoccupations of the Japanese is that at all costs their faces must be saved. On looking around one is given to speculation as to whether this is indeed a prudent resolve. The fact is, the male face of the Japanese could stand improvement if not outright replacement in many cases. The saving of it would seem to me to be unnecessary hoarding. Not so with the women. They are among the most beautiful in the world. Porcelain faces with lips which are a marvel of modeling. Figures like willow wands and the whole drenched in a kind of lambent dew of gentleness. This I regard as worth saving. Even saving up for.

That night we were to have dinner at a Japanese restaurant. We set forth eager to learn, to observe and, in my own case, to eat. The taxi, driven by a homicidal maniac who appeared to have opened hostilities against the world in general, hurtled to a stop outside a heavy stone arch leading into a delightful garden. At the flight of steps on the far side we left our shoes, which lay in line with an assortment of other footwear. We were then given mules in which we flapped eagerly down numerous corridors, past a lot of low doors outside of which lay other people's mules. Finally we arrived at the door of our allotted room, where we duly divested ourselves of the mules and advanced with a disconcerting feeling of nudity in our bare feet.

The room was small and austere and what with this and my bareness I had the distinct impression of being in a very tidy whorehouse.

It was only a fleeting thought as I became at once occupied by the present crisis with which I had to grapple. This was the rather involved process of lowering myself to the floor on which we were to sit. The table was probably fully six inches high and not actually designed to accommodate anyone much over five feet. Being a man of some ingenuity I accomplished the feat with considerable grace and the lady opposite seemed perfectly disposed to let my legs remain neatly arranged where I put them. Which is to say in her lap.

I sat, or rather lay, quietly for a while, notwithstanding some remarks referring to a state of catalepsy into which I had supposedly fallen subsequent to my exertions. I felt them to be in poor taste and anyway was recruiting my strength for the feast to come. Also my first move had proved to be an ill-judged one as I had been severely burned trying, unsuccessfully, to eat what turned out to be an extraordinarily hot towel.

Presently several colorful and kimonoed young ladies came into the room. They made a very interesting entrance

—emerging through the sliding door they at once fell on their knees and then doubled up into a bow from which they never really recovered. The meal was served from this womblike position and combined with my own supine one created the impression of eating breakfast in bed with everyone getting in along with the tray.

The meal opened on a striking note. Nice bowls of raw fish. Before we had finished this, more bowls were brought at the bottom of which lay four lima beans. I think the main charm of this otherwise unpretentious dish lay in the sporting pursuit involved in catching the recalcitrant beans with chopsticks. It was only because of my condition, which was rapidly deteriorating into one of extreme weakness through hunger, that I was finally driven to the more practical, if less native, method of spearing them. Always one to share my triumphs I hastened to reveal this system to the lady on my right and with great skill ate three of hers by way of educating her. She struck a rather jarring note I thought by putting away the last one in her fingers in a very vulgar way, glaring at me with unconcealed hostility at the same time. And all this in spite of the fact that I had only recently married her. One cannot foresee what character flaws may be revealed under stresses of this nature.

Various other dishes arrived in triumphant succession. I remember one consisted of two round flat pink things and there was some speculation as to whether they should be eaten or sewn on. I ate them anyway, although they did look, and indeed taste, rather like cloth-covered buttons.

The whole meal was of course washed down with sake. Although perhaps the word washed is not entirely suitable for a drink which for some inscrutable reason is served in a vessel indistinguishable from a golf tee. The East however, as we have always been told, is full of mystery.

The proceedings had now become so divorced from what

we customarily regard as reality that it was without surprise I noticed the entrance of a new young lady whose folded position in no way detracted from her purposeful air, and who proceeded to uncoil a sizable length of rubber hose she had brought in with her.

I assumed we were to be given a high colonic, and it seemed only to redound to my credit as a well-rounded traveler that I was at once struck by the wisdom of this plan. As every engineer knows, the efficiency of an internal combustion engine depends upon the ratio between input and output. Moreover it was clearly the logical conclusion to the astounding meal with which we had been afflicted.

However, the tubing was intended for no such salutary purpose but was only a gas pipe attachment for the cooking device where the head lady was now moodily simmering the sleeve of her kimono.

Then the entertainers arrived. Four ladies came, or rather crept, into the room which by this time was so full it had the air of wild improbability one used to find only in Marx Brothers films! We all exchanged deep bows and the ladies favored us with their careful scrutiny interspersed with trills of laughter showing that we were clearly a hilarious success as far as they were concerned. This view turned out to be largely unilateral.

After a bit they began their act. One started by letting out some very astonishing bleats which not only caused us considerable distress but seemed to depress her as well, since she closed her eyes and appeared to be in a very advanced state of melancholia. This condition of things was not greatly enlivened by a second lady, who brought out a stringed instrument over which she manifested almost no control at all. Whatever effect this may have been having on us, it managed to galvanize the last two performers into action, and tearing their attention away from us they started to dance. Well, anyhow, they got to their feet which, considering the voluminous kimonos in which they were so charmingly wrapped, and the fact that there was only about four square inches left unoccupied, was in itself quite a feat.

When the performance finally drew to a close it was to tumultuous applause—in which appreciation and relief were rather unevenly combined as far as I was concerned.

We returned to our hotel greatly satisfied by the knowledge that we had been enriched with a new experience and given much food for thought—if not much food.

I was agreeably surprised that the woman in the adjacent bed had at least shown the foresight to pack some chocolate. This in some measure compensated for the unpardonable stinginess with which she had behaved over her wretched beans.

Curiously, our appetite for local color had not been satiated by our first Japanese meal and a few days later we took in the kabuki theatre. It was in an immense and splendid building with a vast stage shaped like a Cinerama screen. The curtain was a magnificent affair of brilliant colors and gold thread which really knocked your eye out and the scenes and clothes were superbly designed. Having said that, I feel it is necessary to add that a lifetime in Europe and America is not really a good background from which to appreciate this kind of thing. Over the years one builds up a frame of reference and various situations strike one as tragic, noble, sentimental, funny or hilarious. The kabuki definitely falls into the last category from a Western point of view. So it is idle to point out the subtle colors and graceful movements to me.

I am hopelessly convulsed by a little man who is sitting up in a sort of cage—and quite right too—letting out the most improbable noises to the anguished accompaniment of his accomplice who has brought a really terrible instrument with him. Furthermore practically anything that happens on the stage will set them off. They have pretty stiff competition from another fellow crouching in the prompt corner who has some hollow pieces of wood with which he plays a lot of galloping-horse-type games. These become particularly frenzied when the main actor is committing harakiri which, incidently, turns out to be one of the slowest methods of suicide yet devised and takes a good half act to bring to a satisfactory conclusion. At one point he even seemed to have a nice chance of recovering, having temporarily overlooked the fact that the sword was still waving bloodily from his midriff as he launched into some particularly vigorous speeches. It is all very strange and incomprehensible. Well, it's absolute hell really.

I realize of course that as an Englishman I am in no position to criticize another nation's adherence to tradition. One could, for instance, imagine a Japanese thinking it irrational to have Buckingham Palace adorned with two boxes containing immobile men buttoned tightly into scarlet coats and balancing bearskins on their heads. It looks perfectly normal, even necessary, to me, but one must in fairness admit the possibility of another view being taken by people not conditioned to that kind of thing.

Fortunately our sight-seeing had now to be curtailed as I was expected to start work. We spent the first week of shooting on the *Ile de France* in Osaka Harbor. It was a strange experience to board the great derelict vessel stripped and filthy, manned by a skeleton Japanese crew, furnished now with the heavy cables and arc lights of the movies and sparsely populated with film extras.

One of the first shots necessitated launching a lifeboat. This was not quite the slick operation one usually associates with the exercise. It took about four grueling hours of enormous physical endeavor accompanied by extensive commands, advice, imprecations and countercommands, all heavily laced with ill-feeling. Rust had welded the boat to its supports; acetylene torches were applied, and when they achieved their purpose a cable snapped, spreading alarm and injuries on all sides.

At this point the Japanese captain of the enterprise arrived on the scene. He must have topped around three foot five in his socks, which he was not given to wearing, favoring a more informal type of dress. He immediately began conferring with the man at the nose of the craft while the man of the stern winch, evidently galvanized by the appearance of his august superior, struck a last titanic blow which freed the boat of its bonds so that it swung out. Well, actually, the stern swung out which somehow resulted in the bow swinging in, where it struck a glancing but very effective blow in the small of the conferring captain's back. This shot him like a bullet into the stomach of his vis-à-vis and the two of them took off in a graceful arc across the deck, landing heavily among a group of extras. This caused a good deal of dissatisfaction all around and a sizable fist fight began to brew.

In the meanwhile the boat, finding itself at last freely abandoned and uncared for, evidently decided to end it all and plummeted nose down to the ocean, ejecting as it went a startled sailor who had shown the poor judgment to suppose that a lifeboat might indeed save his life.

It was fortunate that at this point luncheon was called, thus diverting everyone from his misfortunes. The captain, vaulting lightly under a railing, disappeared followed by his harassed crew, and our own motley group went gaily off to the dining room. One hopes the sailor enjoyed his swim.

It having been agreed that the lifeboats were perfectly unlaunchable, the company addressed itself to other things.

Shots blowing up the ship and drowning the actors occupied the rest of the week.

Meanwhile the Japanese captain and his cohorts of the junk company, who were now the owners of the ship, were given plenty of time, since we were at anchor during this period, for any other intellectual excursions in which they might see fit to indulge, and they developed some highly profitable schemes. So profitable in fact that it was touch and go whether the boat or the film would get junked first.

The morning when we were to leave the harbor and sail for the island of Sumoto dawned tranquil and clear and everyone was on deck at seven o'clock to applaud the take-off. Seeing the mood of happy anticipation was properly set, the captain suddenly appeared from behind a deck chair and strolled over to our director.

"Too bad," he said with an unruffled calm matched only by the waters of the bay. "Can't sail today, too windy." The interpreter delivered this ultimatum to a stunned company. I looked at my cigarette: the smoke rose vertically, taking my eyes up to the yardarm where the signal flag hung limp in the motionless air.

Our director, Andrew Stone, seized the interpreter by the arm. "Tell him we have to sail!" he bellowed.

The news was duly forwarded to the captain. He smiled sunnily, made a modest bow, and with the satisfied air of one who has just concluded a fine performance withdrew to his quarters.

Consternation was on every face. The movie team gathered around the director where they talked for a while in an angry clump. Presently they peeled off and with one accord filed toward a door upon which a piece of white paper bore the inscription *Captain Room*. Several of the junkyard tycoons were inside cosily enjoying a cup of tea. They radiated good spirits.

"Come in," cried the captain, stepping out from under the desk, and with that the battle was joined.

They argued angrily and apparently with no success for about an hour, and then the atmosphere began to change. The intoxicating possibility of a free-for-all was obviously presenting itself to the exasperated movie-makers. There was a pause in the conversation and the air was full of menace. The captain apparently sensed that the time had come for his next move.

"Of course we could sail," he murmured shyly, "if we had three more tugs—even in this wind." He raised a deprecating hand toward the tranquillity of the day.

The interpreter interpreted.

"Get them," said the director. "Get the damned tugs."

"They come," confided the captain, "from the other side of the bay and cost more." He sighed. The interpreter sighed.

"Get them!" shouted the director.

"One has to give notice ahead of time," said the captain. "Unless it is an emergency call which costs more."

"More," said the interpreter.

"How much more?" said the director.

"*Three* times more," said the captain and without benefit of the interpreter. He seemed suddenly to have acquired a fine grasp of the language.

The director appeared to age considerably.

"Get them," he said hoarsely. "How long will it take?"

The captain picked up his megaphone. "I call them now," he said briskly. "They are standing by."

As frustrating as these experiences were, it would be naïve to assume that we would have fared any better if we had been doing business with unprincipled western junk dealers.

There are all kinds of people to be found in every country, but in Japan there seem to be more of them. It is curious that the Japanese people interpret their population problem in terms of the scarcity of land at their disposal. They really have quite enough land. What they need is fewer people.

CHAPTER 9

ACCORDING TO THE PEOPLE who make it their business to study such matters, the net increase in the population growth throughout the world is in the neighborhood of one hundred thousand hungry mouths per day.

Every year, in terms of population, a country the size of Italy is added to an earth that rather stubbornly remains the same size.

Sooner or later something's got to give. In New York there are unmistakable signs that it is beginning to give already. The latest beehive-like Apartment House Skyscrapers are being erected according to designs which permit a maximum of head-room in their living units or cubicles sufficient only for a man of average height. A tall man has to stoop.

The dining room has already disappeared from modern architectural design. Departmentalized living has gone out of style with man's growing poverty and the ever-increasing

182

cost of space. It has been replaced by what are called areas. There are living areas, dining areas and sleeping areas, all of which are merely up-to-date sounding phrases intended to disguise the somewhat unpalatable fact that modern man can only afford to live in one room. Of course, as long as the bathroom remains a separate unit the illusion that a single room is an apartment can be preserved, but in time this too will have to go and be replaced by a general clean-up area in which there would be located a super-absolutely-all-purpose I.B.M. cleansing machine.

It has been calculated that in a hundred years' time the exploding population will have reached the point where an atomic war will become absolutely mandatory. For there will be standing room only. There will be no food because man will be standing on the soil where it grows.

Sex-starved spinsters will at last come into their own. Their laudable continence will become the subject of high-flown hymns of praise sung by Salvation Armies whose main activity will be the distribution of saltpeter and contraceptives.

Broadway play titles would, no doubt, reflect the anxieties underlying the changing cultural values of the times.

Elizabeth and Essex would become *Elizabeth and No Sex* and *Tea and Sympathy* might reappear as *Cocoa and Continence*. Then there would be *French Letter to Three Wives* and *Don't Kiss Me Kate*.

Song titles and slogans would undergo a corresponding change. Among the most popular would be "I Can Give You Anything BUT *Love Baby*" and "Why be half safe when BEODORALL can make you absolutely repellent?"

And so perhaps it is time to consider the problem of how to make a better world. Everyone has a solution, and I am no exception; on the contrary, I am firmly convinced that mine is the only practical one.

Advances in the science of Biological Warfare (Disease Bombs, Nerve Gas, etc.) are only seldom mentioned in the press. Generally speaking, B.W. is considered to be beneath human contempt: several degrees lower than B.O. It has none of the glamour and forthright probity of the H-bomb. It is a sneaky, knavish, nigger in the woodpile kind of warfare, and yet it may spawn the solution to all our problems.

Nerve Gas is said to be tasteless, odorless, and invisible. Its function is to cause people who inhale it to feel rather muddled and dopey and to lose their will to fight. In the event of a modern war it is needless to say that both sides would immediately drop such bombs upon one another and all fighting would thereupon cease. Or, rather, it would fail to get started. Now imagine a few other ingredients added to this bomb. It is not enough for people to feel muddled and dopey—they must also feel high. About three and a half martinis' worth of highness would be my prescription. This ingredient must be added to the bomb.

Now since we have been able to produce disease bombs, surely it is only a matter of time before we will be able to produce health bombs which could be combined with the super Nerve Gas bombs so that then we would feel muddled, dopey, high, and well.

Then why not Contraceptive Gas Bombs?

The much-vaunted oral contraceptive is something people might forget to take for reasons of scruple, or theological superstition. A contraceptive gas is the thing! If we could get the girls to relax, by freeing them from their gnawing fears of pregnancy, and at the same time assuage the anxieties of the men who worry about population growth, we would create a climate for romance in which the very greatest heights of love-making could be reached.

And isn't it better to be exhausted from making love than from making war? I don't know what the moralists would have to say about this but it seems to me that if God is love then love-making must be godly.

I suggest that the Ministers of War of the various countries of the world should henceforth be called Ministers of Love, and that when the government of one country became really angry and hot under the collar with the government of another, its President would declare love on the country in question in the same pompous way that he would normally declare war.

"In spite of all our efforts to maintain peace," he would say over the radio, "the enemy has persisted in its intransigent attitude, and has pointedly ignored my ultimatum. It therefore becomes my duty to declare that a state of love exists between our two countries, and that it will continue to exist until such time as either one or the other reaches a state of complete exhaustion and begs for terms of unconditional surrender."

The National Anthem would then be played, the gas bombs would be dropped, everyone would become muddled, dopey, high, and well. All the latent hostilities of the people would be released and transferred into a gushing torrent of concupiscence.

Then, over the airways of the world, would be heard the booming voice of the great Prime Minister of the defending country.

"We shall make love upon the beaches. We shall make love in the fields and in the streets. We shall make love in the hills, and in the hamlets, and in the towns, and behind the towns; we shall never surrender. And if our empire lasts a thousand years let it be said of us: 'This was their finest hour!' "

After only a few days—no longer than would be required to fight an atomic war—there would come an end to sextilities. Bugles would sound "The Last Kiss" and both sides would go back to work and to a period of peace during which they would restore their vigor along with the gross national product.

The vanquished would build memorials to their Love-Dead—those who responded with excessive zeal to the call of duty—and the victors would savor their successful campaigns to the full, unencumbered by the burdens of Marshall Plan type economic grants for material recovery, since no destruction would have taken place.

This, believe me gentle reader, is the only true road to Utopia. It is up to you and me and all the little people like us to see it through. Do not delay. Act now. Call your congressman. Read once again the stirring words of Shakespeare:

> In peace there's nothing more becomes a man
> As modest stillness and humility:
> But when the blast of LOVE blows in our ears,
> Then imitate the action of the tiger.
> Stiffen the sinews and summon up the blood.
> I see you stand like greyhounds in the slips,
> Straining upon the start. The game's afoot:
> Follow your spirit; and, upon this charge
> Cry "God for Harry! England and Saint George!"

CHAPTER **10**

I N OCTOBER OF LAST YEAR my loyal and de-
voted agent of twenty-five years' standing—William Shiffrin—
negotiated a deal for me to play the lead in a picture called
Bluebeard's Ten Honeymoons opposite Corinne Calvet. The
picture was to be shot at the New Elstree Studios in London.

I remember that some years ago Hollywood's great director
Billy Wilder made a picture called *Bluebeard's Eighth Wife,*
starring Gary Cooper and Claudette Colbert, and I assumed
that this was going to be some sort of remake.

When I heard that the director was going to be none other
than Willie Wilder, I was convinced.

When I heard that the cast was to include Monroe and
Mansfield, I was enthusiastic.

I must confess I found it rather hard to believe that Corinne
Calvet was to be billed above Monroe and Mansfield, but since
it has never been my practice to pay attention to the box-office

fluctuations of Hollywood luminaries, I didn't allow the matter to exercise my mind.

It was not until I arrived in London that I was to discover that Willie Wilder was Billy Wilder's brother, and that the cast, headed by Calvet, consisted not of Marilyn and Jayne, but of Elizabeth Monroe and Violet Mansfield imperceptibly supporting a number of professionally moribund actresses, all of whom, in one way or another, I was to murder during the course of the picture.

It seemed to me that in a way I was being called upon to perform a service to the community that newspaper critics for all their efforts had still been unable to achieve.

On the first day of shooting I was escorted to my dressing room down a long corridor through the producer's building where the names on the doors were really quite impressive.

There was the silver door of N. B. Mayer, and the golden gates of Nevil B. de Mille.

My escort opened the door of my dressing room. "I hope you will find this comfortable," he said hospitably. "Knowing your predilection for relaxing at the piano, we have hired a baby grand Steinway for you."

I thanked him profusely and wandered over to the instrument, which had a fine polish on it. I lifted the keyboard lid —I thought I might as well start relaxing right away. The piano had quite a good tone. I looked up from the keyboard to see the maker's name on the inside of the lid. It was by now without surprise that I read the name STEINWEG.

My relaxation was soon interrupted by a knock on the door and the appearance of the assistant director, who informed me that my presence was required on the set, where I was to meet the director and Miss Calvet and start rehearsing the first scene of the day's shooting.

I took a quick glance at the first two pages of the script and made my way down to the set. Long years of experience had prepared me for the conversation that ensued.

There is an unwritten law in the picture business that all observations and expressed opinions must be replete with superlatives. Generally speaking you can't go wrong if you make sure to use the word "sensational" at least once in every sentence.

The director met me at the door of the stage with outstretched arms and beaming face.

"George!" he cried.

"Willie!" I responded in like tone, and we embraced. We had of course never set eyes on one another before, but in the picture business one makes a point of being friendly at the beginning of a venture.

"What did you think of the script?" said Willie.

"Sensational," I said.

"What about that scene where you—"

"Sensational," I said.

"Why don't you wait until I've finished the question?" said Willie rather testily. "How do you know which scene I'm talking about?"

"I don't need to," I said. "Every scene in the picture is sensational; the whole script is sensational."

He thawed.

He beamed.

We were buddies.

"Okay, everybody," said Willie in a loud and happy voice, "let's rehearse the first scene."

A dark, sober-faced young man stepped forward from the shadows. "Miss Calvet doesn't like her dress," he said.

"So what's that to you?" said Willie.

"I'm Miss Calvet's agent," said the dark young man. "I'm here to protect her interests."

A wardrobe woman was hastily summoned and a lively

discussion took place in which I had no part and which I did not overhear, but it evidently resulted in a satisfactory solution, for Miss Calvet and Willie soon returned, all smiles, and the dark young man receded into the shadows.

The rehearsal proceeded uneventfully and we succeeded in making a couple of shots, but when we came to the close-ups, Miss Calvet found something else to complain about. "I have to protect myself," she whispered to me confidentially as the dark young man sprang forward from the shadows to do battle by her side.

I began to envy all this protection and wondered if perhaps I wasn't missing out on something myself. Yet I must confess that while I had ample opportunity to study Miss Calvet during the shooting of the picture, I never succeeded in discovering just what it was that she was so anxious to protect.

After the first few trials of strength had been made, the picture settled down to a comfortable and smooth routine which lasted all of three weeks, at the end of which time I received a rather disturbing cable from my accountant. I was reading it when I ran into Willie, who was emerging from a projection room where he had been looking at the previous day's rushes.

"How were the rushes?" I asked him.

"Sensational," he said.

"And that bit where I—"

"Sensational," he said.

"Why don't you let me finish the question?" I said. "How do you know which bit I meant?"

"I don't have to," he said. "Everything you do in the picture is sensational—your whole performance is sensational."

"Well, if you are pleased with my work, then how about paying me my salary?" I said, handing him the cable.

"You are definitely entitled to it," he said with deep conviction. "I will send some cables."

He turned and started to walk toward the administration building as a dark figure detached itself from the shadows and approached him. "Miss Calvet doesn't like the dialogue in the next scene," I could hear him saying as I went back to the perusal of my script.

Presently Willie returned with a very important-looking gentleman in tow.

"Let me introduce the president of our company Mr. Lemuel Goldwyn," he said. We bowed. "Mr. Goldwyn definitely thinks that you are entitled to your salary, he is going to send some cables—we are both going to send some cables, and in the meantime if you want a small advance . . ."

"Miss Calvet doesn't like the song you want her to sing," said a voice from the shadows.

"I think I shall send some cables myself," I said and walked away in the direction of my dressing room.

As I walked I mused upon the wacky nature of our business. It is not for nothing that we are the butt of so many humorous jibes. Yet however wacky we may be, at least we can say that we are harmless. We may bore some while we entertain others, but we injure no one. Ours is an innocuous profession. We do not depress the economy with costly strikes. Other workers, such as those in the Steel Industry, should learn our motto: *The show must go on;* it applies more to them than to us. We work whether our employers can pay us or not. We give of ourselves more generously than any other group of people in the world. By virtue of Benefit performances and actual cash donations actors have contributed countless millions to deserving causes. Yet moralists more or less emasculate us, parasitical business managers take advantage of us, critics humiliate and destroy us, and still we have triumphed.

In the face of hostility and opposition that would have staggered lesser men we have succeeded in creating an art out of movie-making. And as Maugham says:

> Art is the only thing that matters. In comparison with art, wealth and rank and power are not worth a row of pins. We are the people who count. We give the world significance. You are only our raw material.